THE ULTIMATE BUSHCRAFT SURVIVAL MANUAL

OUTDOORLIFE

THE ULTIMATE BUSHCRAFT SURVIVAL MANUAL

TIM MACWELCH and the Editors of Outdoor Life

weldon**owen**

To my brother in bushcraft, PAUL DISNEY:
Thank you for the gift of your friendship, and thank you
for the countless hours you have spent planning, researching,
collecting materials, and teaching bushcraft at my school.
I am deeply grateful for everything you have done to help me.

And to my brother in wilderness, MARK HENDRICKS:
Thank you for your friendship and support, and thank you so much
for the amazing photographs you took for this book. Through your
photos, you share your unique view of the natural world, with the eye of
an artist and soul of a poet. I wish you all the success in the world.

CONTENTS

FINER THINGS

Fire

Plants

Animal Foods

9 BUSHCRAFT USES FOR ANTLERS

LONG TERM LIVING

GO WILD

That's the imperative of this useful, smart, relevant guide to the ultimate expression of self-reliance: live by your own skills. Author Tim MacWelch isn't satisfied with simply helping you survive, though. He intends you to thrive in places beyond the reach of cellular signals, power lines, and our imaginations.

You could say this book is a throwback, a guide to ancient knowledge shared by our ancestors before we had electricity, wheels, or even writing. But these skills don't feel old-fashioned. They feel surprisingly fresh—and relevant—in a world built upon increasingly fragile systems.

Besides, what 21st-century human doesn't want to know how to build a wickiup shelter, or catch fish bare handed? MacWelch riffs on several primitive skills, adding a modern perspective about which survival gear to bring or leave behind, how to hunt within the limits of the law, and how to signal for help.

There's no better guide to this world of the back-of-beyond than MacWelch, who preaches what he lives. A longtime survival-school instructor, he is *Outdoor Life* magazine's survival expert, and the person you want along when it comes to foraging, first-aid, wilderness navigation, and a good joke at the right time.

Every guide needs a starting point. At *Outdoor Life*, we hope your first step is one you take off the beaten path, with this book guiding each step you take.

—Andrew McKean, Editor-in-Chief of *Outdoor Life*

Ever wondered if you could hack it in the wild, with just a few well-chosen tools or nothing at all? It can be done and we are the living proof. If our ancestors didn't succeed at the task of surviving in the wilderness, we wouldn't be here talking about it—but it's never been easy. It takes knowledge, skill, and talent to live off the land. This is a book about that kind of survival, but it's also a blend of history and philosophy. Here you'll learn about primitive survival techniques for their historical value *and* as a set of last-ditch plans for survival when your gear is gone. And we'll explore the philosophy of the bushcraft movement. If you're unfamiliar with the term, don't worry. It's not witchcraft or "arts and crafts." Bushcraft is all about thriving in your native environment: the great outdoors.

The basic components of bushcraft are familiar enough. Fire-making and shelter-building are part of the overall skill set. So are foraging and water procurement. And cooking over the open fire is a big deal to many bushcrafters. But the whole point of the bushcraft mindset is a little bit different from the typical mentality of wilderness survival enthusiasts. In wilderness survival, you learn and practice skills that will keep you alive during an emergency in the wilderness—and the end goal is to get out of the wilderness. But in bushcraft, you'll develop and use skills that aren't just helping you survive. They are fun and fulfilling heritage skills that just happen to be helpful in an outdoor emergency. The goal of the bushcrafter isn't to get out of the wilderness, but to venture deeper into it. Bushcraft is more than just avoiding death in the wild. It is the art of being at home (and comfortable) in the wild! And so we begin.

—Tim MacWelch

BARE
NECESSITIES

This first chapter is intended to provide you with a strong foundation in bushcraft and primitive survival skills. We'll delve deep into shelter, water, and signaling for help—the bare necessities you'd need to survive a short-term wilderness emergency. You'll discover that you really can build a shelter with just your bare hands, find water in every terrain, and signal for help with low-tech techniques. We'll also go beyond these basic elements for survival, by addressing the preparation and tools you'd need for all of your outdoor adventures. This is your first step to living off the land as our ancestors once did. It's a step backward in time, and also a step closer to self-reliance in the wild.

PREPARATION

Before venturing out into the wilderness, even the most skilled among us should take some basic safety precautions. And while you may be able to spend the rest of your days living comfortably in the wild with just this book and your trusty knife, don't skip these initial pages. They'll increase your chances of survival. It's been said that fortune favors the bold, but I say that fortune favors the prepared.

001 BEGIN WITH THE BASICS

Any and every excursion into the wild should begin with these steps, at the very least. Your life may very literally depend on it.

HAVE A PLAN Don't just head off blindly into the wilderness. Plan your destination, route, proposed parking area, vehicle of choice, companions (if any), and most importantly your return date and time.

SHARE YOUR PLAN Make sure that someone knows all of the details of your plan. This way, if you don't contact them by the appointed time they'll know that you're in trouble and will have the information they need to help.

GET ORIENTED Study a map of the location you will be exploring, and bring the map and compass with you. Learning the terrain and its features ahead of time makes navigation smoother (and you're less likely to get lost).

DRESS THE PART Wear appropriate clothing and outerwear—layers, wool, and synthetics are ideal. Skip cotton in most conditions.

TAKE YOUR PHONE A charged mobile phone should always be part of your outdoor gear. Your call for help can turn a potential disaster into a mere inconvenience. And if the signal is weak, try a text message. Text often works in spots where phone calls can't connect.

CARRY A KIT Bring a survival kit on every outing. It should include items for shelter, signaling, fire making, water procurement, first aid, navigation, spare outerwear, and food.

BRING A FRIEND It's more fun to have adventures with a friend, and with even one companion, you have someone to watch your back, render first aid, or go for help.

WATCH THE WEATHER Get the most accurate weather forecast before you head out, and stay vigilant. An unexpected change in the weather can turn a pleasant campout into a dangerous situation.

LEARN FIRST AID With even a little first-aid training you can respond to many minor and even major incidents—even if you don't have many supplies to work with.

PRACTICE, PRACTICE, PRACTICE You can learn a lot from watching survival videos and reading books like this one, but there's a big difference between spectator and participant. Gain your own personal experience, and you'll be able to carry it for the rest of your days.

002 GET YOUR PRIORITIES STRAIGHT

For the best chance of surviving an emergency in the backcountry, you have prioritize your needs. For example, exposure can kill you faster than dehydration, so you should find or build a shelter before you wander off looking for water. The four most basic priorities are shelter, water, fire, and food—in that order. And while you could sustain yourself without it, I consider signaling to be the fifth survival priority. You'll need to know how to signal your distress if you're expecting rescue, and especially if you're unable to move.

SHELTER

We'll get into more detail about shelter in the pages that follow, but one of the most basic options is to create a nest of natural materials, like sticks, grass, and leaves. Think of the nests you have seen in nature, and build one to your size. Create a small one that you can just barely squeeze into, and make it thick and fluffy to fight the colder weather or open and breezy if it's hot.

WATER

You'll need to source some water on day one. Look for natural springs, a common way to get reasonably safe drinking water without any tools or materials. But don't start drinking water out of puddles and streams without disinfecting it—that's a fast track to potentially deadly dysentery. Hopefully, you have a metal container in your survival kit to boil water, or you can find bottles and cans to use for boiling.

FIRE

Fire is essential for boiling water, cooking, heat, and light, as well as a signal for help. Carry multiple fire-starting methods with you, as well as tinder (cotton balls, dryer lint, birch bark, or even greasy snack chips) for cold or damp occasions.

FOOD

In a multiday ordeal, you'll probably spend much of your time looking for food. If you're not sure about local edible plants, stick with animal foods. Fish, worms, crickets, and many other critters are safe to eat— but cook them thoroughly, as many of them are loaded with parasites or pathogens. Try to find calorie-dense foods like fatty animals, tree nuts, bone marrow, and organ meats.

SIGNALING

While not as popular to practice as fire making, shelter building, or other survival staples, signaling is your ticket home. Survival kits should have a whistle and signaling mirror, and a smoky fire may be the best signal of all.

003 STAY POSITIVE

While it doesn't keep you alive in the same ways as shelter and water, an upbeat positive attitude and a generous streak of mental toughness can be literal lifesavers in some dire circumstances. The nights are usually the worst time during emergencies. It's just you and your thoughts. When you find yourself at a low point, try to find little ways to maintain your morale and remain motivated to survive. Think of family, friends, and other loved ones, and fight to stay alive— not just for yourself, but for them as well.

004 DEAL WITH DANGER

There are some additional priorities in certain situations, especially when you're facing danger to life or limb.

PLAY DOCTOR Severe bleeding, difficulty breathing, shock, and many other conditions can kill a person faster than exposure, so first aid then becomes more important than shelter in the short run. Without a first-aid kit, effective medical care is much more difficult—but it's not impossible! In this book you'll learn how to practice medicine as our ancestors once did, using what you have and making what you need. Then, follow the other survival priorities to keep your patient (or yourself) alive until you can reach definitive medical care.

DEFEND YOURSELF Rarely, self-defense may be your first priority. Without going into all the frightening scenarios, let's just say that you might run into a person or group that means you harm. You'll need more than we can provide within this book, but consider the weapons and training you'd need for that encounter. You may also run into an animal predator. Bear spray is a proven and trusted deterrent for most animals, and it should be carried in an easy-access holster (just like a gun) in bear country.

005 DRESS FOR THE OCCASION

Clothing is our portable protection from the extremes of the environment (it does a fine job protecting against embarrassment too). And while I'm the first person to admit that I'm the last person to give out fashion advice, I do know my fabrics. Many people get into trouble by choosing the wrong articles of clothing for their outdoor activities. Case in point: long johns. Plenty of companies produce cotton fiber long underwear, which make very comfortable pajamas at home but are actually a dangerous base layer for the outdoors. Cotton fibers hold water for a long time, and when damp clothing is right against your skin in cold weather—it makes you even colder! So if it's cold enough to want long johns, they should never be cotton material. So what should you wear? We're glad you asked.

006 KEEP THE COLD AT BAY

While every season is tricky in its own way, winter weather is definitely the most challenging when it comes to planning what to wear and pack.

The recommendations at right are your absolute basics, but the colder your surroundings are, the more care you'll want to take in packing. The tradeoff of a slightly bulkier pack is not so bad when compared to a case of frostbite!

AT THE FOOT OF IT ALL Wear insulated boots and thick wool (or synthetic) socks. In deep cold, buy boots one size too big to allow for two pairs of socks.

NECK AND NECK Neck gaiters and balaclavas are very nice to have, allowing you to protect against insidious chilly winds.

EYE PROTECTION Sunglasses or dark goggles protect your eyes from snow blindness in bright sun, and can also protect against icy winds.

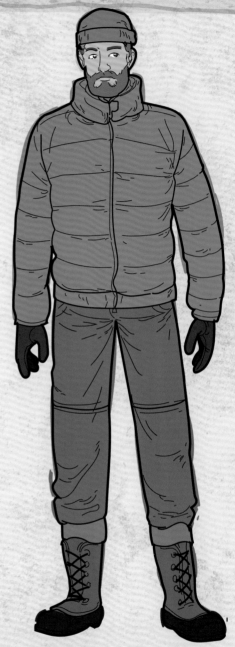

COLD WEATHER

BASE LAYER: Synthetic fabric underwear and long underwear. Long sleeves are a must.
MID LAYER: Wool or synthetic pants and shirt, with an extra sweater or synthetic hooded sweatshirt.
OUTER LAYER: Hooded parka with synthetic fill. A waterproof shell is a plus. Waterproof snow pants over trousers in wet conditions.
EXTRAS: Insulated boots and gloves and thick socks are a must.

MODERATE NICE WEATHER

BASE LAYER: Synthetic fabric underwear
MID LAYER: Midweight wool or synthetic pants, synthetic T-shirt and/or lightweight shirt
OUTER LAYER: Rain gear, as needed. Sturdy hiking boots and synthetic socks. Hat of your choice
EXTRAS: Work gloves. A jacket for nighttime or cold snaps—a packable nylon jacket is lightweight and compact.

HOT WEATHER

BASE LAYER: Synthetic fabric underwear, though you could also use cotton in the tropics. These can be boiled to kill fungus.
MID LAYER: Synthetic pants and shirt. Select thin fabrics, loose fit, light color and keep skin covered for added sun protection.
OUTER LAYER: Rain gear as needed. Breathable hiking footwear and synthetic socks. Add a thin liner sock to avoid blisters.
EXTRAS: Sunglasses, wide-brimmed hat, and thin work gloves.

007 BUILD YOUR SURVIVAL KIT

Even with a high degree of primitive survival and bushcraft skills, you still need to carry a survival kit. It's hard to survive if you are ill or hurt. Injury and illness level the playing field, leaving you just as vulnerable as a novice outdoor enthusiast. Beginner or expert, here's a basic breakdown of the gear you need to be carrying.

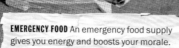

EMERGENCY FOOD An emergency food supply gives you energy and boosts your morale.

1

METAL CONTAINER Pack a metal cup, bowl, or pot to boil water and cook food.

2

SHELTER Carry an emergency shelter item like a Mylar space blanket or an emergency bivy. This may be the most important item in your kit.

3

LIGHTING A rugged, waterproof flashlight or headlamp with an LED bulb can give you over 100 hours of light on one set of batteries.

4

FIRE STARTERS If nothing else, bring a butane lighter for your kit. But you're better off bringing a lighter, waterproof matches, *and* a spark rod.

FISHING GEAR A small kit can be a lifesaver when your food runs out.

SIGNAL EQUIPMENT The whistle signals your buddies or calls for help; the signal mirror can be seen at a great distance.

FIRST AID KIT Carry supplies to stop bleeding, treat wounds, and prevent infection.

NAVIGATION Bring a compass and a map of the local area.

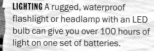

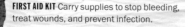

WATER SUPPLIES Water purification tablets (and a container) give you an alternative to boiling all water for safety.

REPAIR SUPPLIES If you can't fix it with duct tape and 550 cord (aka paracord), then you don't need it for survival.

KNIVES Carry a quality knife for dozens of obvious reasons, and bring a backup blade in case of loss or breakage.

008

BRING THE BARE MINIMUM

If you're looking for a minimalist approach to survival gear, grab the first four items in our gallery. A space blanket, headlamp, lighter, and metal cup will take you pretty far. Of course, your chances of survival will go up when you have more tools to work with, but the bare minimum is better than nothing.

❶ The metal cup lets you boil water to make it safe to drink.

❷ The Mylar blanket will quite likely keep you from freezing to death.

❸ The headlamp gives you light and you can even use it to signal for help at night by flashing the light.

❹ The lighter will give you a lifesaving fire.

009

GO REALLY OLD SCHOOL

Our ancestors didn't have access to high-tech solutions. But they did carry a simple kit to help them survive. You can do the same.

SHELTER A canvas tarp soaked with waterproofing oils or waxes makes a good roof for your shelter.

BEDROLL Wool blankets stay warm, even when wet.

COOK KIT A metal pot with a bail handle for hanging over the fire will suffice.

FIRE KIT Pack flint and steel, matches, or another historic fire-starting method, plus tinder.

TOOLS A knife and some cordage will get you pretty far.

CANDLES Beeswax burns the longest, so it's your best bet.

FOOD Basic staples like cornmeal, sugar, and shortening can make some great meals.

AXE AND SAW You'll rely on these essential tools for building your camp, and cutting and splitting your firewood.

010 KNOW YOUR KNIFE TYPES

Knives are categorized by their design—they may be created for hunting, combat, survival, bushcraft, and many other tasks. Other major differentiations are the blade material and hafting techniques. Other considerations including the shape of the blade, tang, and edge, are discussed below. Obviously, there are a lot of variables. So whatever knife you choose, ensure it satisfies your needs.

EASY TO SHARPEN So what if your knife is razor sharp right out of the box, if you can't field-sharpen it to a razor edge again? Find a knife that is easy to sharpen with a basic whetstone.

A GREAT GRIP It doesn't matter if your knife handle is Micarta, glass-reinforced nylon, or a chunk of deer antler. It needs to offer you a solid and comfortable grip, wet or dry.

SUITS THE TASKS Select your blade according to the jobs it will need to perform for you.

011 RECOGNIZE BASIC BLADE STYLES

Blades come in a variety of shapes and designs, each with their own advantages. Here's a look at some of the most common.

DROP POINT Good all-around knife.

TRAILING POINT Good for skinning and filleting game.

MODIFIED TRAILING POINT Good for skinning and slicing.

STRAIGHT BACK Good for applying pressure to increase cutting power.

SPEAR POINT Good for piercing work, skinning, and drilling holes.

STRAIGHT EDGE Good for controlled cutting; easy to sharpen.

CLIP POINT Good for cutting in tight places, and fine detail work with the point.

012 CHECK THE TANG

The tang is the back part of the blade metal that extends into the handle. Is it skinny like a rat-tail tang or through tang? Or is it a full tang? If you plan to beat your knife with a baton to split wood, you'll need a knife with a full tang. Many bushcrafters prefer smaller woodcarving knifes made from Mora steel for camp chores and woodworking, though they typically have weaker rat-tail tangs. Here are your options.

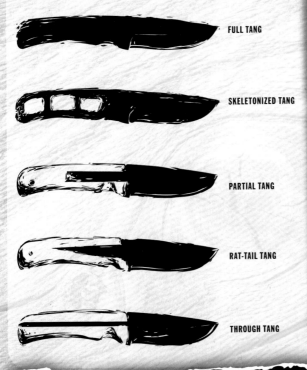

FULL TANG

SKELETONIZED TANG

PARTIAL TANG

RAT-TAIL TANG

THROUGH TANG

014 CUT SAFELY

Your knife is an indispensable, even mandatory tool for wilderness survival, and you need to know how to use it properly and safely.

+ Always cut away from your own body, and away from others.

+ Always keep your knife sheathed when not in use.

+ Don't keep your elbows on your thighs or hips when carving in a seated position. Keep your elbows on your knees. This trick prevents dangerous cuts to your artery-filled legs.

+ Never rush your cuts or "hack" at the wood. Every cut should be controlled.

+ Don't allow others in your "blood circle" (this is the circular space around your body that could be reached with your knife blade).

013 GET TO THE EDGE

You'll want to consider the geometry of the knife edge. For example, the Scandi is excellent for carving, while a full convex edge is great for chopping and heavy work. Edge types in between offer differing amounts of durability and finesse in your work.

SCANDI   HOLLOW   HIGH FLAT   FULL FLAT   FULL CONVEX

015 SHARPEN WITH A ROCK

Don't have a sharpening kit? Don't worry. You can literally sharpen your knife on a handy rock, which could be a vital skill in the wild. I'd even go as far to say that being able to restore a keen edge to your knife is almost as important as carrying the knife in the first place. Here's how you can make a shaving-sharp edge.

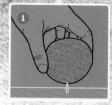

STEP 1 Look for a fine-grained round stone in your local waterways. Select one that has a smooth section, and seems similar in texture to your normal sharpening stones.

STEP 2 Check how dull your knife really is. Look for nicks in the edge, and try cutting a piece of paper or rope to test it. If the knife won't cut well, or it has deep nicks in the edge, you have a lot of sharpening ahead of you.

STEP 3 Apply some water to the stone and sharpen you knife with little circular strokes, equal numbers for each side of the blade. Hold the knife at a 45 degree angle, then lower it by half. In a perfect world, this would be 22.5 degrees, but close enough is good enough. For a 4-inch (10-cm) blade, do about 30 little circles on each side, maintaining the described edge angle as best as you can.

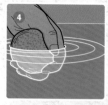

STEP 4 Rinse your stone often while sharpening to keep the stone's pores open so it keeps cutting steel. Do several rounds of sharpening to each side of the blade.

STEP 5 Once you feel you've sharpened enough, remove burs and polish the edge by stropping the blade against a leather belt or log (or even your pants if you're careful).

STEP 6 Test the edge with a small carving or slicing task. If you're not satisfied, sharpen and strop again. And if you were wondering, all of these steps can be used with modern store-bought sharpening supplies as well.

016 MAKE AN EMERGENCY BONE KNIFE

Lost your cutting tool? That's a shame, but you still have a fighting chance if you know how to make a replacement for your sharp cutting tool. Later in this book, we'll show you how to make stone blades that are actually sharper than steel knives. But for right now, here's a trick to tide you over. Find a leg bone from a medium sized animal, say a wolf or small deer. Tap the bone slightly with a rock until it begins to show many hairline fractures. Twist the bone hard and you'll get a unique break—the spiral fracture! Find the resulting sharp edges, and use the bone piece as a knife. It's not as sharp or durable as steel, but it will serve until you can make a better blade.

017 WET YOUR WHETSTONE

Don't let the similar words confuse you. The word "whet" means "to sharpen," not "to moisten." And while you may actually commonly apply water or oil to a whetstone when sharpening your blades, you can also use your stones dry. Just brush or blow off the dust periodically, to keep the pores of the stone open, and they will continue to cut steel for you.

018 GRAB THE RIGHT SAW

Does anyone but a lumberjack actually carry a saw out into the woods? Yes, and here's why. Saws can cut wood, bone, and antler very quickly and cleanly. The metal saw blade is an amazing invention that dates back to 3000 BCE, when the ancient Egyptians used copper saws to cut wood and even stone. Later saws were made from bronze, then iron, and finally steel. Flexible modern steel blades are very efficient, and a great help in the wild. Even if you're traveling light, there are still lightweight saws you can carry. For bushcraft, we can focus on three groups: pruning saws. bow saws, and bucksaws.

PRUNING SAWS Scoff if you like, but pruning saws are great lightweight camp saws. They are designed to cut both dead dry wood and wet live green wood, softwood and hardwood. Pruning saws are available as fixed-blade and compact folding models.

BOW SAWS With its bow-shaped handle, this saw can be used for cutting branches and small logs, or larger softwood logs. Bow saws have a thin lightweight blade and generally a light frame.

BUCKSAWS Need something that's built to last and capable of cutting all kinds of wood? Think of the bucksaw as a people-powered chain saw.

019 CHIP A SHELL SAW

Coastal and riverine areas hold an amazing array of ecosystems, and within this variety, you'll find many helpful resources. Take the shell for example. Bivalve shells can provide us with a great resource for survival (made even better if there is still a tasty clam or oyster inside). Use a small stone to chip at the edge of a shell, pushing from the inner (concave) side of the shell toward the outer (convex) side. When pushing this direction, chips of shell will break off leaving a sharp toothed edge that you can use for cutting tasks. Shell saws aren't usually sharp enough to cut rope, fabric or leather, but they will cut vegetation, softwood, and meat. Shell saws are great for cutting grass to make bedding or shelters, and this tool saves your knife from dulling due to the silica present in all grasses.

020 BUILD YOUR OWN SURVIVAL BUCKSAW

It will take a few well-chosen parts to put your survival bucksaw together.

- A knife (to do some notch carving)
- A saw blade. A bucksaw blade is best, as it's wider and stronger, but a bow saw blade will also work.
- Four sticks: 2 thicker ones for uprights, 1 crosspiece, and 1 windlass. The lengths will vary, depending on your saw blade.
- 550 cord (twice the length of your saw blade)
- Two small nails
- Two hardwood pegs (you'll cut to fit)

A BUILD THE HANDLES Use your two stout sticks as the handle pieces. Saw a slot in the bottom of each handle piece to receive the saw blade. You can use your bare blade (carefully) to cut the two slots.

B ADD THE CROSSBAR Start to drive a nail into the center of each handle piece, lining up each nail in the same direction as the saw cuts. Drive the nails until they're just poking through the handle sticks. Line the nails up with your crosspiece and hammer them into place. Your handle pieces and crosspiece should look like a squatty "H."

C FINISH THE JOB Now cut notches at the top and bottom of each handle piece (on the outside of the "H"). Drive small hardwood pegs through the holes at each end of the saw blade, and seat the pegs in the bottom "H" frame notches. Loop the 550 cord around the top notches of the saw frame, place the windlass in the looped cord, and start tightening the windlass. Tuck the windlass behind the crosspiece when the blade is nice and tight. Your saw is now complete and ready to use!

021 SAW SAFELY

Nothing cuts wood across the grain as quickly and efficiently as a sharp saw. But those sharp teeth can take a bite out of the sawyer too, and there's not likely to be a doctor out there in the woods if you saw your finger off. Use these tips to stay safe when wrestling with a beast that has more teeth than you do.

COVER UP Keep a cover on your saw blade when you're not using it.

REACH THROUGH If you have to hold logs or branches to steady them while sawing, reach through "open" saws like bow saws and bucksaws to hold the wood. This way, your hand and forearm are inside the saw opening and thus cannot be cut by the saw teeth.

STEADY ON When steadying branches to cut them with a handsaw (like a pruning saw), reach over the saw's spine to hold the branch you're cutting. This protects you just like reaching through an open saw.

GET SUPPORT Support the wood you are sawing so that a shifting log doesn't pinch the saw blade.

EASY DOES IT Start sawing slowly, unless you're in some kind of lumberjack contest.

022 KEEP IT CUTTING

Like any other tool, saws require care and maintenance to stay sharp and useful. These steps should keep your saw in top form.

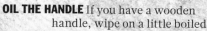

KEEP IT DRY Store your saw in a dry place or a moisture-free tool box to prevent rust.

LUBRICATE THE BLADE After each use, lubricate your blade with gun oil, paste wax, or WD-40 before storing. Gun oil or WD-40 can be wiped on with a rag. Paste wax should be wiped off after sitting on the blade for minutes. All of these choices prevent rust and help the saw blade slide through wood.

OIL THE HANDLE If you have a wooden handle, wipe on a little boiled linseed oil periodically to seal it off from moisture and dirt. If your handle shows rust where it attaches to the blade, take the handle apart and clean out the slot. Use medium-grade steel wool or fine sandpaper to smooth a rough finish on the handle and remove stains (then finish with oil).

REMOVE BLADE RUST A well-maintained blade may never rust, but if it does, a razor blade can help. Remove the handle and lay the blade on a flat work surface. Scrape the saw blade carefully with a razor blade, going up and down the length of the blade and keeping the razor at a low angle. Scrub any stubborn spots with medium steel wool or 320-grit sandpaper, especially the handle area. Wipe with a soft, dry cloth, and then oil or wax the blade immediately.

023 STAY SHARP

Saw sharpening can be tricky for beginners, but it's well worth learning since it can keep a quality saw blade in service for years. You'll need a small triangular or diamond file, suited to the saw teeth. It's also helpful to clean the saw blade as previously mentioned and work where you have good lighting.

STEP 1 Work your way down the blade, filing each tooth bevel and counting strokes as you would for knife sharpening. You'll need to make more file strokes if the blade is very dull, and fewer strokes if you're just maintaining it. Do your best to match the factory angle on the saw tooth bevels.

STEP 2 Make sure all the teeth are the same length. File down any longer teeth, or they'll be doing more than their share of work.

STEP 3 If your saw blade has rakers, give them a check. These are like notched teeth, and they should clean up the cut made by the saw tooth next to it. You should file your rakers sharp, and make sure they are all a tiny bit shorter than the saw teeth (otherwise they will bog down the blade).

STEP 4 Finally, check your blade for bent teeth. Many types of saw teeth are bent outward and twisted slightly so that they make a wider cut than the thickness of the blade (to keep the blade from binding). If any teeth are bent out of shape, do your best to bend them back to the blade's pattern (you'll often need a special setting tool for this task).

024 PACK A BACKUP

You'll often see something called a "survival saw" or wire saw, a toothed or abrasive piece of wire that can be pulled back and forth to cut smaller wood and branches. They can be coiled up and stored easily, but keep wire saws stretched out as straight as possible while using them. Wrapping the saw completely around a branch to cut it will cause stress to the wire and break it much more quickly.

For the heavily muscled woodcutter, there's the pocket chain saw. This upgraded version of the wire saw actually uses a modified chain saw chain, which you pull back and forth to cut wood. This engineless chain saw is quiet and needs no gasoline, though it is strenuous to use. The task gets easier, however, when you add a wooden handle to your wire saw or chain saw (just as you would for the DIY bucksaw).

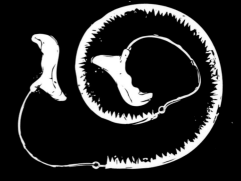

025 MAINTAIN YOUR AXE

When maintaining an axe, you're really caring for two different materials—the metal axe head and the wooden axe handle. Your main chores with the axe head are rust removal and prevention, and sharpening the edge of the axe. A little rust is inevitable, and this can be easily removed by scouring the axe head with steel wool. Once cleaned, apply a thin coating of gun oil to prevent future rust. Other oils will work. In fact, the pioneers used pig fat or beeswax to protect their tools, but gun oil is your best bet. It will dry somewhat once it's applied and it's long-lasting. Your axe handle can be cleaned with a quick scouring of steel wool or fine-grit sandpaper. The handle's useful life can be extended with an occasional wipe of boiled linseed oil. Make sure you choose boiled linseed oil, not the raw version, as raw linseed oil leaves a sticky residue that will not dry. A final handle chore involves the hafting. If an axe head becomes loose, you can try adjusting the wedges that hold it in place, but your best choice is to remove the wedge and rework or replace the handle.

026 SHARPEN THAT AXE

A dull axe edge can be a dangerous liability, as you have to swing the axe harder to make your cuts. This is even more treacherous when you are way out in the woods where an axe mishap could leave you seriously injured and far from help. Lucky for us, axe sharpening is not much different than knife sharpening; in fact it's often easier. Axe and hatchet blades don't require such a delicate touch as knife blades.

A FILE ONE AWAY Start by sharpening a nicked or seriously dull axe with a file. Don't sharpen "into" the blade (from sharp edge toward the handle), as this causes you to risk pushing the file too far and cutting yourself. Rather, file from the back of the axe head, toward the edge and out. This creates more of a burr than filing the other way, but it's faster to remove a burr than regrow a fingertip. Work both sides of the axe equally, counting strokes. File until the blade edge is beginning to feel sharp again and any chips or nicks in the edge have been eliminated.

B MOVE TO THE STONES Once you're done with any necessary filing, use a whetstone. I prefer to work against a stationary stone. Lubricate it with oil or water as you normally would—use water if you're not sure what your stone likes to drink. Go in little circles, from one side of the edge to the other, counting strokes and matching that on the other side. If the blade has a burr, whetstone the side with the bur until it is gone, then sharpen each side with equal strokes.

027 HANG AN AXE HEAD

If you use axes, sooner or later you'll need to replace an axe handle. And in some circles, the only right way to replace a handle is by "hanging a head."

STEP 1 Clean the hole in the axe head, and file away any rough edges. Place the axe head near a fire while you go to work on the handle. Heat it until it's hot to the touch, but not hot enough to burn your hands.

STEP 2 Sand the end of the new handle to a very snug fit in the very warm axe head.

STEP 3 Hand-fit the axe head on the handle, so it barely sticks on there.

STEP 4 Hold the end of the new handle, with the barely-stuck-on axe head dangling near the ground, but not touching anything.

STEP 5 Tap the free end of the axe handle with a hammer—and then prepare to be startled by physics. Because of the mass, the axe head tends to hang in midair as the wooden axe handle drives down into it. You'd expect the axe head to fall off, but it creeps up the handle a little further with each blow. Hammer the handle until it emerges from the other side of the axe head. Drive in a wedge to lock the handle in place. It's best to do this while the axe head is hot, as the metal is expanded. When it cools and shrinks, the head will be even more secure.

028 BE AXE AWARE

A good axe or hatchet can be a major player in camp life. This tool proves us with high-quality, split firewood and saves us a lot of labor and time. It can help with specialized tasks, such as bow making, bowl carving, and making camp furniture. But be careful! The axe is also one of the most dangerous tools in the woods.

✚ Don't swing an axe downward in a "circle." If you miss your target, you'll chop into your knee, shin, or foot! Instead, straighten out your swing at the end of the chop and drive the axe into your chopping block. And yes, you should be using a chopping block.

✚ Keep the axe head covered when transporting it. You should also use the cover while staying in camp, instead of leaving the tool lying around or stuck in a tree or a stump.

✚ When cutting branches off a tree, or putting in a notch to fell a tree, never chop upward! A glancing blow can end up driving the axe into your neck, face, or head.

✚ Never swing an axe with a loose head. The axe head may literally fly off the handle and hit someone.

CAVEMAN'S CORNER

029 HACK IT WITH A HAND AXE

You can still chop if you get caught without your steel axe. The oldest and simplest axe is the stone hand axe. Unmodified stones with a natural sharp edge are the most expedient, but if you know how to work stone and have suitable raw material, you can flake your own hand axe. Select a flat stone and chip an edge around it with another stone. Leave an area unworked, for a natural handle, or work the entire edge. Refine the stone until it has a teardrop shape and you're done. Use the tool for chopping and sawing, and save the stone flakes made producing this tool. They work very well as skinning blades or arrowheads.

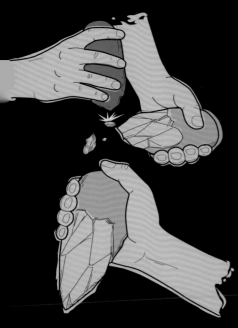

AXE GALLERY

030 PICK THE RIGHT AXE

As with knives, there are many different axes that can help us in the bush. Here are just a few.

❶ **TOMAHAWK** Straight-handled like a maul, these little axes are on the opposite end of the weight spectrum. Feather-light and easy to carry, these tools are designed to be carried on the trail for camp tasks. They have also been devastating weapons when used in hand-to-hand combat or thrown.

❷ **BROAD AXE** Widest of the axes, these have some unique features. Only one side of the axe head is tapered, the other is flat, and its handles

are often offset too. These adaptations help the user chop round logs into square beams.

❸ SPLITTING MAUL These thick and heavy axes, typically with a straight handle, are used for splitting firewood. They were also used to dispatch livestock before the mechanization of slaughterhouses. A blacksmith would draw out the edge to a point, which was meant to strike the livestock between the eyes.

❹ DOUBLE-BIT AXE It may look like a battle axe, but the double-bit axe is actually for felling and limbing trees. One edge is stout, for the hard work of felling; the other edge is sharper, for chopping limbs when the tree is on the ground.

❺ CAMP AXE These small to mid-sized choppers (aka hatchets) are useful for both camping and survival. Lightweight and designed for use in one handed use, they're ideally suited to chopping and splitting small wood. The famous Hudson Bay axe is a great example of this group.

❻ CARVING AXE Generally of higher quality and with a keener edge, carving axes are used in historic carpentry projects and they are excellent for bushcraft tasks.

❼ FELLING AXE Felling axes are made to cut across the wood grain, and are ideal for cutting logs and trees. Once they've dropped the tree, they can be used to "buck" the log (chop it to the desired length section).

031 FELL TREES WITH CARE

Dropping a tree to the ground has many inherent dangers, both to people and property. Just look up "tree felling fails" on the Internet and you'll see pictures of people who have dropped trees on fences, trucks, and even houses. These mishaps are on the lighter side, but people, pets, and livestock have been killed by tree felling, so be sure nothing bad happens on your watch.

+ STUDY UP Understand that every tree is different, so assess each one before the tools come out. Study it carefully to identify lean, cracks, rotten areas, dead branches, dead tops, and other hazards.

+ CHOOSE THE TIME Never try to fell trees on windy days, as these are very dangerous conditions.

+ SUIT UP Wear protective gear and work with a partner nearby, but out of the tree's range.

+ CLEAR THE PATH Clear your work area around the trunk and escape routes before you start. Ensure that you're the only living thing in the area before cutting.

+ TAKE A POSITION Always work with the direction of lean (or the weight, such as with a tree with more branches on one side than the other).

032 LOOK FOR THE LEAN

It's always smart to make some plans before you get out your axe and start chopping. One of the chief plans involves identifying a tree's lean. While some trees are perfectly plumb (straight up and down, and able to drop in any direction), most trees have some slight lean and they need to fall that way. This lean can found by tying a weight on a string and using this as a plumb line, to compare against the tree trunk from multiple directions. Some leans are very obvious, and you won't need a string. But for others, the plumb line will help.

033 CUT CAUTIOUSLY

Once you have determined the direction of lean, you can then make your cuts accordingly, to make sure the tree falls the way that you want it to.

CUT AWAY Start by making the face cut on the side of the lean, about a third of the way through the tree trunk. Next comes the back cut, which should be slightly higher up the trunk and parallel to the face cut. Leave an equal strip of the trunk to act as a hinge for the falling tree.

DRIVE A WEDGE IN Once you finish making the face and back cuts, you might still need to finish the job. Keep a few plastic felling wedges (or wooden wedges) handy, and drive them into the back cut to coax a stubborn tree to fall.

034 PLAN YOUR ESCAPE

You'll need a clear path (away from the falling tree) before you can safely shout the word "Timber!" in the forest. Before you attempt to drop a tree, you'll first want to clear all of the brush, vines, and saplings around the base of the tree, so that you have a clear space to work. Then you'll want to choose two escape paths away from the tree. Your primary path should be away from the anticipated direction of fall, and off-line about 45 degrees from the direction opposite of the intended fall (in case the tree falls backward). While you're at it, have a second path chosen in case you need it.

You probably don't expect much from tree bark. It's rough. It's crusty. It's there to protect the trees, even if it looks like a crumbling suit of armor. But there are hidden virtues in the bark of many tree species, if you know what to do with them. Here are just nine of the many ways that tree bark can serve you in the wild.

❶ ROOFING SHINGLES My Native American ancestors once used large sheets of bark to cover their wigwams and longhouses. These sheets were peeled in the springtime, when the bark is naturally separated from the wood. The sheets were then flattened, dried, and attached as an excellent roofing material. Today, we can scale this down for shelter making, which makes less impact on the environment. Pry off dead bark slabs from fallen trees and work them into the roof of your survival shelter as simple shingles.

❷ TINDER A favorite tinder of mine is tree bark. Once wood has died and become a little bit rotten, the fibrous inner bark can be peeled from many species to yield fire-building tinder. Depending on the area, you may have cedar, juniper, cyprus, basswood, tulip poplar, paw-paw, and many other tree barks to harvest. A quick "pre-test" of bark tinder is the length of fibers that peel free from the dead wood. Generally, the longer (and softer) the fiber strips, the better that bark will be for tinder. Paper strips of birch bark can make great tinder too. Their high oil content allows these strips to burn even when wet.

❸ CORDAGE Most of the long strips of dead inner bark that are good for tinder can also be used for rope, cord, and string. Basswood and mulberry are excellent prospects, yielding strong durable cordage. Tulip poplar and cedar barks can make for midgrade cordage, which is durable if thickly woven. Try your various local bark fibers to find the one that works best for you.

4 FIRST AID You can use bark and cordage to create a temporary splint for an arm or leg. As with all splints, pad the limb heavily for comfort and support. Once you've bound the bark slabs in place with a generous amount of cordage, do your best to immobilize the limb further. This will limit further injury, as well as the pain that comes from movement.

5 CONTAINERS Bark buckets, baskets, and containers can be made from the thin-skinned, flexible barks of birch, tulip poplar, and cedar, among others. From the canoes and maple syrup buckets made from birch in New England, to the bark cooking pots of Australia and Africa, flexible barks can take many shapes.

6 MEDICINE The inner bark of red oak can be chopped from live branches and boiled until the water is brown to release tannic acid for soothing inflamed skin, rashes, ingrown toenails, and many other maladies of the skin. Slippery elm twig bark can be steeped in hot water as a tea and sipped to relieve coughs and sore throat. Black willow twig bark can be scraped and made into tea for pain relief. Just make sure you have positive identification of any tree species you're ingesting.

7 INSULATION The corky, airy nature of most outer tree bark materials can make a natural barrier between you and the cold, wet ground. Collect large, flat, dead slabs of corky bark like locust and oak. Lay them on the ground in your shelter, and then use a thin layer of vegetation on top to soften the bed. Insulating tree bark can also be used in the walls of primitive shelters.

8 UTENSILS Need a plate, a serving platter, or a small paddle to shovel food into your mouth? Bark strips, squares, and rectangles may have been the original version of the paper plates we take for granted today. They may taste a little funny and be single-use items, but they do bring a touch of civility and culture to a savage outdoor feast.

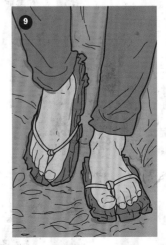

9 FOOTWEAR If you're caught without hiking boots, cut some flexible bark the size of your feet and use cordage to bind them over your toes, like flip-flops, but not past the ball of your foot. Add a retention cord around your ankle if one is needed.

Using rope or cord to tie things together is as old as the hills, and it's an essential skill set for every outdoor adventurer. These are some of the most useful and reliable knots, handy for building camps, traps, and many other necessities in the wilderness.

SQUARE KNOT This is a classic for connecting lines. Whether you are tying two ropes together to make a longer rope, or securing a bundle of firewood to carry, the square knot is a winner. It's much more secure and stable than its common cousin, the "granny" knot. Just make sure you use it with matching diameter and texture ropes (use the sheet bend when joining ropes that are different types or sizes).

SHEET BEND Nothing works better for tying different types of material together and joining different thicknesses of rope. This knot even works with lines or materials that normally couldn't be joined together.

With the sheet bend, you bend the thicker or more slippery rope into a "J" shape (like a fish hook). You then pass the other rope through the fish hook from behind, wrap around the entire fishhook once, and then tuck the smaller line under itself.

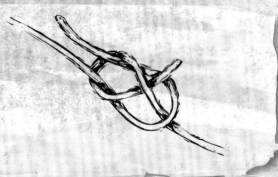

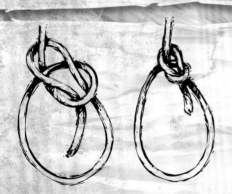

BOWLINE The bowline creates a fixed loop at the end of a rope. This knot is often taught by a story of a rabbit coming out of the hole in front of a tree, going behind the tree, and back down the hole.

Form a loop atop the long end of the line. Pass the free end of the line through the loop from behind. Pass the end around the standing line and bring it down in the original loop, while maintaining the secondary loop which becomes your bowline loop. Once the "rabbit" is back down his hole, pull the "tree" up and the bowline is tightened.

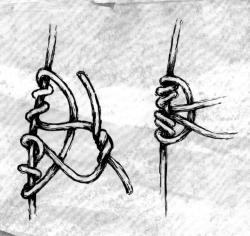

PRUSIK KNOT The Prusik creates a loop that can be used as an ascender or descender. This "slide and grip" knot is also very handy for adding a loop to a rope when neither end is free.

Start with a short rope and a separate long rope. Tie a loop in the short rope, secured by a square knot. Wrap the loop around the long rope three times; keep each wrap flat against the long rope. Pass the loop of short rope under itself and pull it tight. As long as there is weight on the loop, the Prusik will grip the long rope. You can also slide it up or down the long rope by taking the weight off and pushing the knot upward or downward.

TIMBER HITCH The timber hitch secures a rope to a cylindrical object for hauling or as a support. This has been used to allow draft animals to pull logs from the forest, and it's the perfect knot for starting a diagonal lashing.

To create a timber hitch, all you need to do is run the free end of the rope around the log you intend to pull. Then wrap the free end of the rope around the standing end of the rope. Wrap the free end around itself four or five times. Finally, tighten the timber hitch so the four or five wraps are tight against the log.

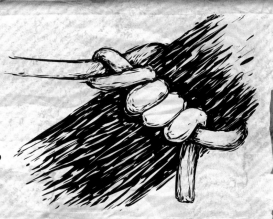

TAUT LINE HITCH The taut line hitch takes the place of a slide lock to tension or loosen a loop in a line (like a tent guy line). This knot grips well, as long as tension is on the "taut" side.

Start a loop by wrapping around something like a tree or tent stake. With the free end of the rope, wrap toward the stake twice. Then wrap the free end of the rope over everything, toward you one time around the rope. Cinch these wraps tight. Pull on the standing line; the taut line hitch should grip the loaded line.

036 LEARN SQUARE LASHING

This is a great way to secure poles that are at right angles to each other; it's used to build everything from camp chairs to towers and bridges—but you can also use it just to secure two poles.

STEP 1 Tie a clove hitch to one pole, near where the two poles cross. Leave several inches of rope free on the tag end of the line (you'll tie back to this later).

STEP 2 Wrap your line around the junction of the two poles, going under the lower pole and over the top pole.

STEP 3 Spiral outward with these wraps four times. This part of the lashing is called the "wrapping." Next, wrap between the poles, biting onto the previous wrappings to tighten them. This part is called the "frapping."

STEP 4 Finally, use a square knot to tie the free end of the rope to the tag end from the clove hitch that started this whole lashing.

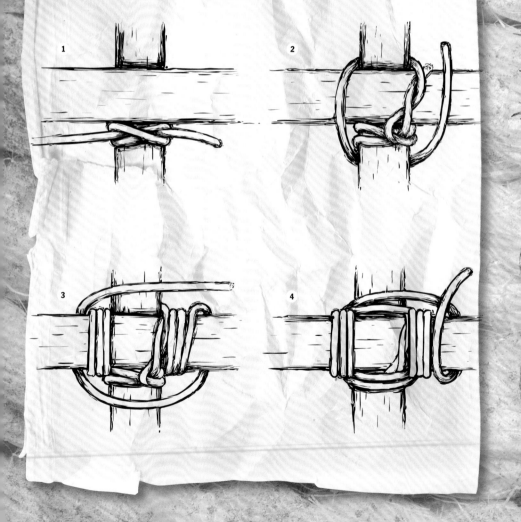

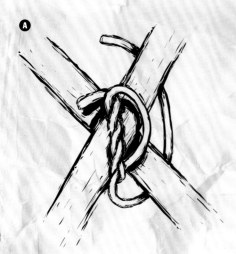

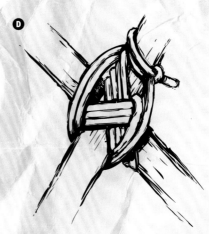

037 TAKE THE DIAGONAL

This lashing is similar to the square lashing, but is best suited for tying together poles not at right angles.

A Tie a timber hitch around both poles, then pull them tightly together.

B Make four wraps vertically around the poles, then another four wraps horizontally around both poles.

C Tighten the lashing with several frapping runs between the poles.

D Finish the lashing by tying the rope to the tag end of your timber hitch, or by tying a square knot around one of the poles.

SHELTER

Shelter is absolutely crucial in the outdoors; it's even more important than food or water. A savvy survivor knows that food is one of the lowest survival priorities, since the average person could last for days with water and weeks without food so long as they have adequate shelter. Your shelter doesn't have to be a palace. There are many ways to keep your body at a nice comfortable temperature in the wild.

038 FIND THE RIGHT LOCATION

If you build a glorious shelter in a bad location, you may have to abandon it. But a few basic guidelines can help you determine a good place to build.

FIND THE RIGHT SPOT Avoid open fields or mountain peaks, or deep in a forest or jungle where it takes longer to dry out. Look for a transition area between habitats. Pick a place clear of anything that could collapse on the shelter, with plenty of building materials.

STAY DRY Choose a well-drained place where no water will get under the shelter. Build on a slight hump in the ground, and avoid gullies, drainages, ditches, and low-lying areas. Don't build next to any body of water, to avoid accidental pollution. Keep the shelter free of dampness, and avoid insects like mosquitos.

CHECK FLORA AND FAUNA Avoid areas with dangerous plants and animals. I also scrape the ground bare to look for anything else that would keep me from using that spot.

BE SAFE Keep fires at least 12 feet (4 m) away from your shelter and downwind of the structure—natural material shelters can catch fire easily.

039 MAKE ANY SHELTER BETTER

Jungle huts, snow caves, and lean-tos may not seem like they have much in common. But they're all shelter, and they have some similar flaws and merits. Use these tips to make any shelter into a more effective, practical, and comfortable home.

PRACTICE YOUR SKILLS The time to try out some new shelter architecture is not during a real emergency. Practice making your shelter before you really need it; this way you'll know exactly what to do.

MARK YOUR TERRITORY Natural shelters are hard to see from a distance. Mark the shelter with a scrap of colored cloth or plastic, so that you can find it again in low visibility and searchers may find your camp in a rescue situation.

FACE THE SUNRISE In the northern hemisphere, face the shelter door to the east or southeast to catch the morning sun and avoid the prevailing wind and storms.

BEAT THE BUGS Shelters can be smoked out to remove insects. Remove the bedding completely and place a fireproof container of coals and rotten wood inside the shelter.

040 ASSESS YOUR ASSETS

The volume and variety of shelter building materials are high in the average forest. If you have an axe or saw in your gear, the only real limits are time, calories, and talent. Without too much trouble, you can find timbers or poles to build sturdy shelter frames. Leafy boughs are abundant in the woods, and bark slabs make great shingles. But bears, widow makers, and other hazards can be found in this tree-filled habitat. Your sunlight and airflow may be limited in a forest too. In most areas, your best plan is to set up your shelter and campsite near the edge of the forest. You will be close to building supplies, but also have more sunlight and air (the forest blocks wind from storms).

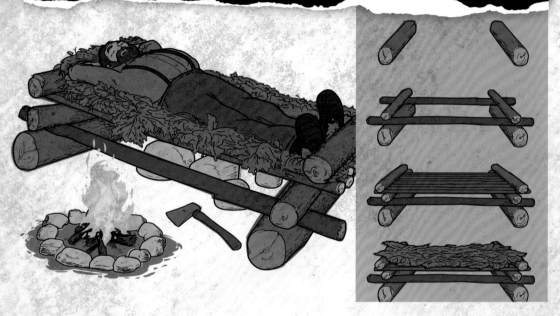

041 BUILD A "SASQUATCH" BED

A bed can really make a camp feel more like a home; lucky for you, a springy "Sasquatch" bed isn't that hard to make. With a little work, you'll be snoring like Bigfoot in no time.

STEP 1 Start with two short, thick logs, about a yard (1 m) long. Set these on the ground under your shelter, a little farther apart than you are tall. Angle them a bit so they open more toward your fire to catch heat more effectively.

STEP 2 Lay two poles on top of your logs, and add another two logs. Drive eight stakes into the ground (two of them in each corner) to hold everything in place.

STEP 3 Add a layer of flexible poles for your mattress frame, and another pair of logs to hold them in place. There should be plenty of room under the bed to place hot stones underneath (without them touching the frame), to keep you warmer on the coldest nights.

STEP 4 Finally, top your mattress frame with soft vegetation for comfort and insulation, and drift off to sleep.

042 MAKE A LEAF HUT

The leaf hut is a wilderness shelter that needs no sleeping bag or fire for warmth, just body heat. This overgrown "people-nest" can protect you from the cold, wind, rain, and snow. It can be made from wet or dry materials, and when properly built it can hold in most of your body heat. Dead air space is the key to its success. As your body heats the air around it, the shelter keeps the warm air from being lost to the environment. And the thick, round dome of debris sheds water and wind, while a frame of sticks and brush keeps everything in its place.

BEAM Select a long, sturdy pole **A** for your beam. It should be at least as big around as your arm, 9 to 12 feet (3 to 4 m) long, and strong enough not hold the shelter's weight.

BEAM SUPPORT This can be a sturdy fork in a tree, a rock, a stump, or a pair of moveable forked sticks **B**. Whatever supports your beam should be about 3 feet (1 m) tall, and tested for strength to avoid shelter collapse.

RIBS Use dead tree branches, thick rigid bark slabs, freshly cut tree boughs, or whatever you happen to have lying about. Place the ribs **C** at an angle along both sides of the shelter beam, and keep the ribs close together so leaves don't fall through.

LEAVES Add insulation—leaves **D** or anything that traps air (grass, ferns, moss, pine needles, brush, and tree boughs) can be used. Green materials can be used, but dead means more insulation for the same amount of material. Three feet (1 m) of leaves protect from wind, rain, and snow, but you can still freeze without proper bedding.

BEDDING Pack insulation in the shelter **E** twice as much underneath as is covering you, with more in the corners to prevent cold spots. A large pile of leaves can be placed outside to be pulled in as a door plug and pillow.

BARK AND BRUSH Bark slabs **F** can be used as shingles for more wind and water resistance (remember, huts are not waterproof). Add a final layer of brush over the dome to keep wind from stripping your leaves away.

043 LEARN THE LEAN-TO

The lean-to is a classic backwoods shelter, and with its odd name, it's often attributed to Native American architects. But this isn't the case. The lean-to (in name and building style) come from the late middle English of Britannia, and it simply means a flat roof that leans up against some other structure or support. The lean-to is not quite as efficient a shelter as one might hope, since it offers little insulation and merely deflects some of the wind. Yet it can be comfortable, if it reflects the heat of the nearby fire. Just remember that when the fire goes out, the warmth goes too. I prefer to use this type of shelter as storage, wind block, workshop, or fire reflector, and use the leaf hut for my sleeping quarters. But to each, his own. Here are the components.

BEAM Select a long, sturdy pole for the main beam. It should be at least as big around as your arm and strong enough not to break under the shelter's weight. The pole can be any length.

BEAM SUPPORTS The beam supports are a pair of sturdy poles 6 feet (2 m) tall with a very sturdy fork at the end of each. These hold the beam up and pin it against two trees, or another stable structure. Find a place where the supports and beam can lean against trees or other structures with the open side facing away from, or at least parallel to, the wind. The beam supports and structures should be tested for strength, using your full body weight. Never try to build a freestanding lean-to against posts or tripods. The one-sided construction makes them dangerous, and very much like a large dead fall.

RIBS These can be dead branches or freshly cut poles, placed against the beam on an angle to shed the rain. Set them up at a 45-degree angle if you expect your roofing to shed water effectively. Set your ribs at a steeper angle (around 60 degrees) if the roofing materials will be leaky (loose, light, or porous). Place these ribs close together so that the leaves or other vegetation won't fall through.

LEAVES Heap leaves or other debris over the frame to block wind and shed the rain. The angle of the lean-to roof naturally sheds water; add bark slabs for even better water resistance. Like the leaf hut, a layer of sticks, twigs, branches, or poles should be placed on the outside to keep the wind from stripping the leaves. Put a heap of leaves under the lean-to, or build a Sasquatch bed (see item 042).

044 MAKE A DIY TARP TENT

With a tarp, a few stakes, some rope, and your choice of trees for support, you can quickly build an A-frame tarp tent and still have time to play Daniel Boone (or Danielle Boone) before supper. Just tie a rope between two trees, estimating the height of your shelter. Orient the rope so that the open ends of the shelter will line up with the wind for a breezy shelter, or set the walls against the wind if conditions are cold or stormy. Flop your tarp over the rope line, and use short ropes to attach the edges of the tarp to stakes that you've driven into the ground. Don't worry, no one ever gets the dimensions perfect on the first try. Just raise or lower the main guy line, adjust the two "tent walls" in or out, and adjust the length of line from the tarp edge to the stakes to finish your shelter. Make sure all knots are tight, and your shelter is done.

RECIPE FOR SUCCESS

045 WATERPROOF CANVAS

Long before there were cheap plastic tarps at every camping store, our progenitors made their own waterproof tarps from the natural materials within reach. This was commonly called "oilcloth" and you can make it too!

THE INGREDIENTS
- A piece of cotton canvas, large enough for your needs
- 1 gallon (4 liters) of boiled linseed oil (or more for big tarps)
- 1 pint (0.5 liters) of dry iron oxide pigment powder or very finely powdered charcoal
- A paint bucket and brush

THE RECIPE
Start by washing your canvas and drying with heat. This will remove dirt and any other undesirables (like fabric sizing product), and it will tighten up the fabric. If you have an indoor space to work in (like an empty garage), you can spread the dried canvas on the floor; otherwise, nail it up on a flat wall or fence.

Mix your linseed oil and your pigment of choice in the paint bucket. Always use boiled linseed oil, as the raw version will never really dry out. Iron oxide pigment (basically rust) has long been used to make a brick-red color called Spanish brown. Or you can use powdered charcoal, which will give you a dark gray color, sometimes called Yankee gray. Paint the exposed side of the canvas with the paintbrush, working the "paint" into the fabric. Allow it to dry for several days, flip it, and paint the other side. Allow the tarp to completely dry (several weeks), and you'll have genuine oilcloth to use for backwoods shelter roofing, a ground cloth, firewood cover, and pretty much anything else you can imagine.

046 CARVE OUT A MICRO-CABIN

If the idea of a log cabin appeals to you (and you're in the forest with an axe), then you can build the sturdiest shelter of them all: a micro-cabin. For ages, people have used timbers to create small, sturdy structures. From the Native American hogans of the southwestern U.S. to the pit huts of the frozen Arctic, log shelters can be as diverse as the people who have used them. Logs offer both strength and thermal mass (both great things in a shelter). Posts and beams are a great way to support the roof; just keep them small so you can work on the roof without a ladder. Wall logs can be set horizontally, with the corners notched, just as a large log cabin would be built. Logs can also be stacked and held in place by stakes driven deep into the ground, though this is not a load-bearing wall. Pack any gaps with moss, mud or a mixture of both to keep the wind out. Make sure that your roof is incredibly well-built and even overengineered to hold weight (there'll be a lot of weight up there). Poles can make your roof, and be covered with vegetation to act as thatching (or a waterproof tarp). You can even add a stone hearth and chimney if you feel ambitious. Make a small doorway, use a blanket to cover it, and you'll be ready to move in!

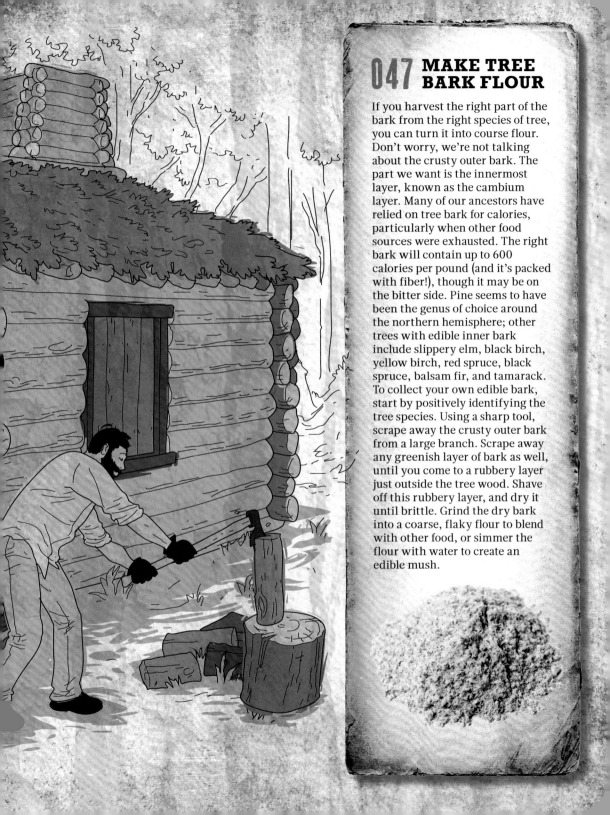

047 MAKE TREE BARK FLOUR

If you harvest the right part of the bark from the right species of tree, you can turn it into course flour. Don't worry, we're not talking about the crusty outer bark. The part we want is the innermost layer, known as the cambium layer. Many of our ancestors have relied on tree bark for calories, particularly when other food sources were exhausted. The right bark will contain up to 600 calories per pound (and it's packed with fiber!), though it may be on the bitter side. Pine seems to have been the genus of choice around the northern hemisphere; other trees with edible inner bark include slippery elm, black birch, yellow birch, red spruce, black spruce, balsam fir, and tamarack. To collect your own edible bark, start by positively identifying the tree species. Using a sharp tool, scrape away the crusty outer bark from a large branch. Scrape away any greenish layer of bark as well, until you come to a rubbery layer just outside the tree wood. Shave off this rubbery layer, and dry it until brittle. Grind the dry bark into a coarse, flaky flour to blend with other food, or simmer the flour with water to create an edible mush.

048 FEEL WELCOME IN THE JUNGLE

You know where you are? You're in the jungle, baby! For those who live, work, vacation, or travel through rainforest environments, having knowledge of jungle shelters is a must. In a biodiverse and life-rich habitat like the jungle, there are always a wealth of resources at your disposal (and plenty of hazards too). Big leaves can make quick waterproof roofing, and fast-growing softwoods are easy to cut for shelter poles and posts. But to carve out a home in this steamy landscape, you'll need some specialized skills and knowledge. There are plenty of plants and animals that you shouldn't even touch (like that colorful little frog). That's not the worst of your troubles either. It gets dark early in the tropical forest, and when it rains, it pours. Then there are the spiders, jaguars, anacondas, and jungle foot rot. You'd better build a top-notch shelter and a big fire, because the sun is on its way down.

049 BUILD YOUR OWN TREE HOUSE

If you can find a jungle tree with two matching lateral branches, you can be the envy of the neighborhood kids by building your very own tree house. Start by placing cut poles across the lateral branches. You'll need thicker poles if they have to span a wide distance, and you can get by with skinnier poles in short spans. You can create a safety rail (always a good idea) by cutting a large forked tree branch and hanging it by ropes or lashing it in place. Add a pole with cut-off branches to use as a ladder, and drape a bug net over the top for protection. As a final defense (which you can do on any raised shelter) tie thorn branches around the tree trunk to discourage snakes and other dangerous animals from climbing up.

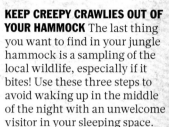

KEEP CREEPY CRAWLIES OUT OF YOUR HAMMOCK The last thing you want to find in your jungle hammock is a sampling of the local wildlife, especially if it bites! Use these three steps to avoid waking up in the middle of the night with an unwelcome visitor in your sleeping space.

STEP 1 Keep it well covered. Things have a tendency to drop out of the trees in the rainforest, and when your hammock is sitting there open like a big basin, it's only natural to find all kinds of creatures raining down upon you. Hang a rain fly over your hammock, even if it's the "dry season."

STEP 2 Limit access. Just as you don't want to lie down on the ground in the jungle, you don't want to have open access points that lots of pests and dangerous creatures could use to join you in your hammock. Don't tie six lines to your rain fly when four will do the job.

STEP 3 Block the way. Tie a kerosene-soaked rag to each hammock line to keep spiders, snakes, and ants from scuttling down the lines to join you in your cozy hammock. Because of the scent and the feel of this fuel, most creatures won't go near it (let alone crawl over it).

Why do so many cultures use hammocks in the jungle, you ask? For starters, they get you up off the wet ground. They can also be quite comfortable. They can get you further away from spiders, scorpions, snakes, and other nasties. The hammock is one of the most underutilized shelters for survival, and you can make it with just a bit of rope and sturdy fabric. Grab some finger-thick rope and two tarps, pick out two strong, young trees, and you're ready to create your own hammock and rain fly. Start out with one of the long sides of one tarp and roll it up halfway across the entire tarp. Then roll up the other long side to meet the first. Now we'll grab one end of this bundle and bend it to make a "J" shape. Tie a sheet bend knot with a length of rope. Using a second rope, tie another sheet bend on the other side of the tarp. Select leg thick or bigger trees about 9 to 12 feet (3 to 4 m) apart, and securely tie the end of each rope to a tree, as high as you can reach. I like to wrap around the tree twice for good grip on the bark, and tie to the trees high up to compensate for the settling of the hammock as the knots cinch down. This keeps you from dragging the ground in the finished hammock. For a roof over your head, tie up another tarp as an A-frame rain fly between the two trees.

051 SURVIVE THE DESERT

You know you're in trouble when you're in a place where the only green plants are armored in spines and needles. There are many kinds of deserts in the world, each with their own challenges and assets. But despite their differences, there are common factors that make them all a hard place to call home. The combination of scarce rainfall, wild temperature swings between day and night, and dangerous wildlife make the desert a harsh terrain unlike any other. In no other place could you die of heat stroke or hypothermia just 12 hours apart. Only the toughest of plants and animals can survive here, and the toughest, luckiest, or best prepared of people.

052 MAKE A WICKIUP

This shelter is found across the globe, but has been most frequently seen in the American Southwest. A wickiup is a small tipi made from poles and brush (instead of buffalo hide). Thick brush and grass, with a steep roof, make it suitable for the occasional desert rain. A broad, squat structure covered in light brush provides a shady, ventilated area in hot, dry climates.

❶ Collect several dozen poles, some with forks at the top. Lock a few forks together for a tripod.

❷ Lay the other poles around the tripod to create the conical tipi frame.

❸ Finish by layering on any vegetation or brush that you have available. If the wickiup is large enough on the inside, and the vegetation you have used for the roof is not especially flammable, it may be safe enough to risk a tiny fire inside this type of shelter—but generally speaking, this shelter provides cool shade instead of warmth.

053 CRAFT A MINI-EARTH LODGE

In days gone by, many Native American tribes and nations allowed the earth to be their home—in the truest sense. Soil-covered structures (later called earth lodges) were once seen throughout the American heartland. We can pay homage to the early architects by building a mini-earth lodge as a cool home in harsh desert climates.

STEP 1 Start by sinking four posts into the ground, and affixing four beams across the top of the posts.

STEP 2 Encircle this log "cube" with poles, as if replicating a tipi-style shelter.

STEP 3 Build a tunnel-like entrance using more posts and beams.

STEP 4 Cover the entire structure with a thick layer of grass, followed by packed soil. This is the most labor-intensive shelter in the book, but it's also capable of lasting a very long time.

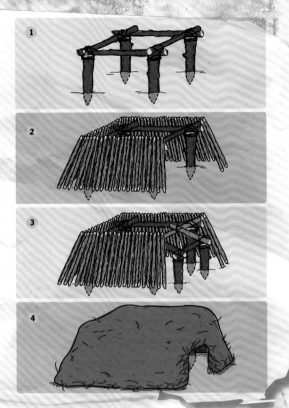

054 MAKE A TWO-TARP SHELTER

This double-roofed shelter dates back centuries among desert cultures, particularly in northern Africa and the Middle East, but it finally found widespread fame through the last century's military survival training. To get started with this shelter, you'll need two tarps, four stakes, and several yards (meters) of rope. Find or dig your own low spot in the ground. Lay one of your tarps out over the low spot and drive in each of your stakes at each corner of the tarp.

Tie your tarp tightly to the stakes, and then tie the other tarp into place, so that it leaves about a foot (30 cm) of air space between the two tarps. You can also fold over a larger single tarp to create the two layers. Tie the tops of the four stakes to four anchors, which can be stakes, rocks, logs, or any other strong anchoring points. Crawl underneath and enjoy temperatures that may be as much as 20°F (–7°C) cooler than the outside.

055 CLIMB EVERY MOUNTAIN

Many mountains are just as treacherous as they are beautiful. Their cold temperatures, unpredictable weather, and limited resources have always restricted the number of people who call the mountains home. But for those who cannot escape the magnetic pull of this striking landscape, it's best to be prepared. Whether you're high up a mountain or just a place where the main resources are soil and rock, you need to know how to use this environment to get the things you need, including shelter. The lucky mountaineer may find a turnkey home in the form of a cave or rock overhang. But those who don't bring a portable shelter with them need to be ready for the grueling work of building shelter from the flesh and bones of the earth—dirt and stone.

056 BUILD A STONE HUT

Moving and lifting stones is backbreaking work, no question about it. That said, a stone hut could last for a very long time and support an indoor fire with greater safety than most other shelters. Here's how I glibly explain this insanely laborious build.

STEP 1 Find a level hut site, with plenty of flat, square, or otherwise blocky stones nearby—very nearby. You can use round stones or cobbles, but they'll yield walls that are far less stable (or just plain dangerous).

STEP 2 Lay out your perimeter and the door location. Plan the height as well. Don't aim for a stone mansion. Plan for something that will fit one bed, as this is achievable, whereas the mansion—not so much.

STEP 3 Start stacking stones. Use mud and grass mixed together as mortar, if needed. Try to find the space where each stone fits best. Don't build any walls taller than yourself, or with any stones that seem to shift; otherwise your stone hut could become a crypt.

STEP 4 Add roof beams, roofing material, and a door, and fill any gaps with mud mortar.

057 BUILD A DIAMOND IN THE ROUGH

This tarp shelter has an aerodynamic wedge that cuts through biting wind and driving rain—common elements in mountainous areas. With its sleek shape and minimum of three attachment points to the ground, the diamond is more secure than most tarp shelters. For even more protection, add another tarp as a door. Stake down one corner of the tarp on the side that the wind is coming from and tie the opposing corner to a tree, post or some other structure (this orients your "door" out of the wind). Pull these tight, and secure the remaining two corners down toward the ground. Add additional tie downs where ever you can.

058 DIG A HOT ROCK HEATING PIT

You can't have a fire in a cave (or many other types of shelters), so it's good to know other ways to heat your living and sleeping area. By digging a small pit in the dirt floor of a shelter, finding a good-sized rock that will fit into the hole, and a flat rock to cover the pit, you have the makings for an in-ground heater. Get your two rocks from a dry location (water-logged rocks explode when heated), dig your pit, and make sure everything fits together well. Heat your stone in a fire, carry it to the pit (a shovel works well), and drop it in. Seal the pit with your flat stone lid, and bask in the radiant heat for several hours to come.

059 SCULPT A SNOW CAVE

Where snow has drifted into deep piles and frozen into a solid mass, you can excavate an excellent shelter with a shovel, large cooking pot, or even your gloved hands. First, dig out your very own snow cave. Then, add some ventilation holes and a "cold well" to give the colder air a place to sink away from your sleeping area. Use a backpack or block of snow for a door. In all snow shelters, pile up a deep mattress of evergreen boughs or other insulating materials for a mattress.

060 USE A TREE WELL SHELTER

In an evergreen forest with deep snow, shelter can be as easy to find as a naturally occurring tree well. These are gaps (or at least areas with less snow accumulation) under the shelter of the area's evergreen trees. When the snow collects on the tree boughs (rather than under the tree), it creates a natural pit that can be quite easily adapted into a shelter. If possible, dig down to the bare ground and use the snow to fill in gaps around the rim of the well. Since a fire down in this shelter would melt the snow-covered boughs overhead, your best bet for warmth is packing the cavity with insulating materials. If you can manage to find a few rocks in the snow, use a nearby fire to warm them and place them in your bedding to serve as heaters.

061 CRAFT A QUINZEE

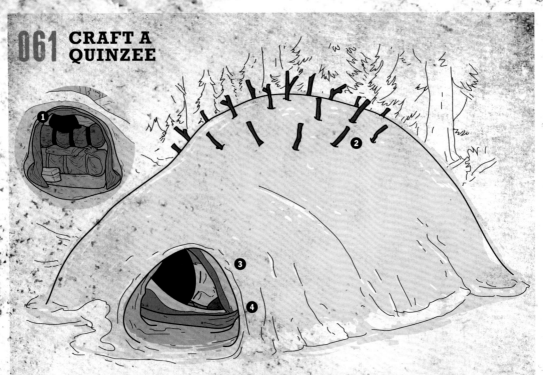

In wet, packable snow, a quinzee makes the most sense for a small group shelter.

❶ These structures are built by piling up some gear (or snow) and covering it with a tarp (if you have one).

❷ Snow is then mounded and packed down on top of this pile and sticks are inserted around the mound. The sticks should all be the same length (about 12 to 18 inches / 30 to 45 cm) and will act as depth gauges. Allow the pile to settle and harden for a few hours, if possible.

❸ Then dig in a doorway, pull out the gear (or the initial snow pile), and excavate as you would for a snow cave. Stop digging when you start to hit the sticks; this will prevent thin spots in the dome which could weaken it.

❹ Add a door and you're ready to spend the night in this "poor man's igloo."

062 DON'T EAT SNOW

Snow is made out of water. And we need water every day. So what happens when you're lost in the snowy wilderness, and out of water to drink? As strange and desperate thoughts swirl like snowflakes in your head, you cautiously place a handful of wet snow in your dry mouth, and revel in its moisture—until the brain freeze hits. Now the problem is revealed. As you chill your mouth, throat, and stomach by eating snow, you're chilling your body core directly. Also, snow is 90 percent air. This means you'd need to eat ten cups of snow to get a cup of thirst-quenching water. This puts you on the fast track to hypothermia. There you have it: eating the white stuff will kill you.

Fighting the cold? Need help cooking? Don't underestimate the power of hot rocks! Stones can hold a lot of heat, and radiate that warmth for a long time when properly insulated. A few caveats: Never use rocks from a wet area, as they may have trapped moisture which can cause them to explode when heated. Similarly, glass-like or crystal-filled stones and slate or shale are prone to explosion and breakage near heat. Just grab some plain old ugly rocks from a high, dry location, heat them up, and enjoy the results.

❶ WARM YOUR BODY Heat a stone near the edge of a camp fire. Make it toasty, but not hot enough to melt your synthetic clothing (or your skin). When the rock is held under a coat or jacket, it can stay warm for about an hour.

❷ WARM YOUR BED For a warm and comfortable night, heat a large, flat stone to about the same temperature as scalding-hot tap water. Wrap it in tough cloth or clothing, and put it in your bed or sleeping bag. The heat will soak into your cold bedding and you'll drift off to a snug night of slumber. I've had rocks remain warm as long as 7 hours this way.

❸ BOIL LIQUIDS Rock boiling can be used to prepare soups and teas, and to boil your water to disinfect it. Collect about two dozen egg-sized or slightly smaller stones to rock boil 2 to 4 quarts of water. Heat them in your fire for 30 to 45 minutes. Use sticks or split-wood tongs to pick up the rocks and drop them into your water. Use one or two at a time, and rotate "cool" ones out and hot ones in.

❹ FRY FOOD For small cooking tasks, chuck a flat rock into the fire for 10 minutes to heat it up. Once hot, slide it out of the fire with a stick and dust off the ashes. Drip a little oil on the stone and set your food on the rock to cook. This is a dead simple way to make delicious fried foods, and you don't even need a frying pan! For a more permanent setup, check out the cooking tips in later pages.

❺ HEAT A SHELTER Get a large fire going (good luck in the blizzard). Heat up one or several large stones. Use a shovel or similar tool to bring them into your shelter and place them on a platform of cold stone. Pile a few cold stones around the hot ones for safety, make sure nothing flammable gets near the hot rocks, and enjoy the radiant heat.

❻ WARM YOUR BONES For sprains, strains, cramps, and other maladies, a warm rock can provide soothing comfort when held against the affected area and can even help to counteract hypothermia (cold exposure that can lead to shock and death). To treat a victim of hypothermia, place a warm stone under each of their armpits and one between their thighs. Wrap them up and repeat the treatment until their body temperature rises.

❼ GO FISHING Want some fresh fish, but the pond is frozen? Simply burn a large fire on the shore and heat up a large stone in the blaze. After an hour of heating, use a shovel to carry the dangerously hot stone to your ice-fishing spot and set it on the ice. It will begin to melt the ice immediately and work its way downward. Soon the rock will melt through the ice and drop into the dark water below. Your ice fishing hole will be open, smooth, and ready to fish.

❽ STEAM A MEAL The steam pit is a truly remarkable cooking method, used around the globe. It's basically a hole in the ground (or a raised mound) with hot rocks at the bottom as a heat source. These rocks are covered with dirt or sand, then a layer of green vegetation with your food on top. The pit is finished with another layer of vegetation and covered with dirt to seal in the steam and heat. After a few hours, your food is tender and cooked through.

❾ SWEAT IT OUT A natural sweat lodge functions like a sauna, for relaxation and cleanliness. Place hot stones in a small enclosed space (like a tiny hut), dribble water on the rocks, and enjoy the waves of steam. Don't overdo it. If you feel dizzy, open up the lodge for fresh air. Towel off when you're done, drink lots of cool water, and you'll feel squeaky clean and rejuvenated.

063 TEST YOUR ROCKS

If you're uncertain about the stones you find, toss some samples into the center of a large fire and go 20 yards (meters) away. Wait 30 minutes, watching and listening to the fire at a distance. If the rocks are going to explode, they'll probably pop in the first 10 or 15 minutes. Even if they don't explode, some rocks may just crumble into sand. This is less dangerous, but still not useful. After the fire dies out, examine the rocks left. Their color has likely changed, but if they seem whole, you have a good type of rock for boiling. And, you could still heat them by the fire for hand warmers.

WATER

Water is an absolute necessity for life, and in the wild, we have to put in work for each and every drink we take. But it's not always a dire struggle to stay hydrated. Water can be found in a surprising number of places, and disinfected in many different ways. Take this section to heart, and you'll never take water for granted again.

064 PLAN TO PROVIDE

Most of us grab a bottle of water before we head out the door, but are we planning far enough ahead? Follow these tips, and diminish the threat of dehydration.

BRING IT ALONG Always take water with you, and more than you think you'll need when trekking through dry locations. It is heavy to lug along, but it's an essential effort.

PREPARE TO DISINFECT Disinfection tablets, a commercially produced water filter, and a metal pot to boil water in are reliable tools to help you eliminate pathogens in your drinking water. As with other critical supplies like shelter items and fire starters, you should carry multiple pieces of water-disinfection gear. Redundancy virtually guarantees you'll have something to work with during a predicament. One to break, one to lose, one to use.

KEEP AN EYE OUT As you go through the landscape, look for water. Just because your trail map shows a blue line representing a creek or spring, this doesn't guarantee that water will be present. Sometimes the only available water comes from unexpected and undesirable sources. I know, muddy water and swamp water taste terrible, but this is survival—you're not on some bottled spring water taste-test panel.

065 FIND YOUR WATER

Want some advice about finding water? I'll give it to you straight: Just walk downhill. That's right—across 90 percent of the landmasses in the world, you can find surface water after taking a hike downhill.

This is the path rain takes; rivers, springs, and creeks are all headed down too. In flat areas, you can still do the trick of walking downhill to look for water, and if the land is open, you can look for water-favoring trees and plants at a distance to guide your path. Willow trees, sycamores, cattails, sedges, cordgrass, and reeds are a good sign just about everywhere.

The larger a waterway is, the more time it has had to pick up pollutants. Find a smaller source that pours into it. All water gathered from the landscape should be purified if at all possible.

In dryer and more rugged terrain, finding water gets a lot harder. Check the base of cliffs or hills, where the groundwater table is being pulled upward. Look for gorges and ravines where rainfall may evaporate at a slower pace. Depending on the geology, you may even be forced to look around for water on high ground. Certain areas are full of rock depressions called "kettles," which can hold water in higher ground, where no streams or other sources may be easily found.

066 HARVEST PRECIPITATION

If there's not a nice spring or lake nearby, water can also be collected in various forms of precipitation.

RAIN This is the most efficient source of clean water, clean as the air it formed in and the surfaces it has touched. It requires no further purification if you catch it in a clean container under an open sky since it is fresh, distilled water. In a jungle or forest, I disinfect rainwater that I have collected under the canopy. All those tree leaves and branches are the bathroom for all the birds and bugs that live up there. After a long rainfall with no disinfection methods available, I would consider the canopy "washed off" and drink rain collected underneath (again, with no other option). But it should still be disinfected if at all possible.

SNOW The frozen stuff requires more consideration than rain, as it needs to be melted and perhaps disinfected. Fresh snow is likely safe but old snow could be contaminated. Don't eat snow; it takes ten quarts to make a quart of water and eating snow leads to hypothermia. Melt the snow in a pot near a fire; sleet and hail can be collected similarly.

DEW AND FROST Other forms of precipitation can be collected for water. Dew is only as clean as the surface it collects on, so it should always be disinfected. Dew and frost are best collected before and around sunrise in low lying areas. It can be sopped up with a piece of absorbent cloth, a sponge, or a bundle of dried grass. Wipe up the dirty water, squeeze it into a container, then boil it or chemically treat it for safety.

067 DIG FOR A DRINK

How do you find water when none is at the surface? When your hike downhill hasn't panned out, find the lowest, dampest spot you can and commence digging.

GO UP A CREEK It is not unheard of to find water in the soil of dry creek beds and other low-lying areas. If you do hit moist soil, keep digging. The hole should soon start to collect muddy water. Once water starts to appear, let the moisture seep into the hole and allow the mud to settle.

HIT THE DUNES Another good place to dig for water is at a beach. Even if no freshwater streams seem at first glance to be flowing into the ocean, experiment by digging holes beyond the beach dunes. In the low spot behind the first or second dune, dig down until you barely hit water. You may find a layer of freshwater on top of the salty groundwater. This is rainwater that has been preserved, since the dry sand above it prevented evaporation. This doesn't work everywhere and at every time of day. The high and low tide can impact the presence of freshwater. So experiment with the depth, location, and timing of your "rain well" and taste-test for salt. If it's even half as salty tasting as sea water, find another spot or don't dig as deeply.

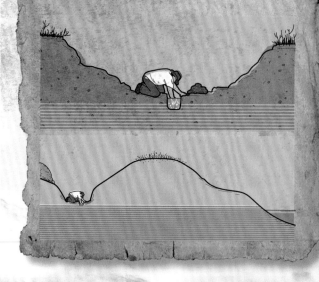

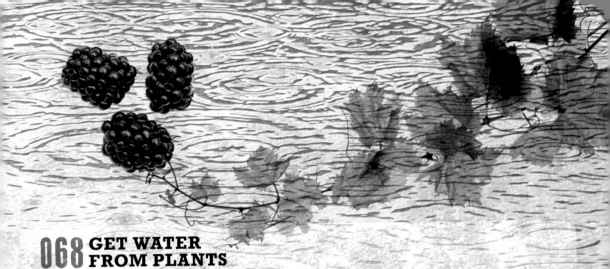

068 GET WATER FROM PLANTS

If we've learned anything about the wild from watching cartoons, it's that we can chop the top off a cactus and have a cool drink of water in the desert. Bad news: It doesn't work like that. Cacti have moisture inside just like every plant, but not liquid water. However, the cartoon artists weren't too far off. Some plants and trees really can be sources of water at certain times of year. This is seasonal and shouldn't be relied upon, but when it does work, it's amazing. Water from plants usually doesn't require purification, although it never hurts to be safe. Here's a breakdown of when and how to get water from plants.

THISTLE Many different species of thistle are scattered across the northern hemisphere, with plenty in North America. There are no toxic species in the U.S., just a few bitter-tasting ones. Before the flower heads of a thistle start to swell in early summer, you can scrape off the sharp spines from the immature stalk and munch on it for a celery-like treat, or just chew it for the water it contains. It takes several stalks to get even a few ounces of water, but by chewing the stem and swallowing only the juice, you're getting water.

TREE SAP Maple trees have a watery sap that is used to make maple syrup and is safe to drink (except the introduced Norway maple, which has milky toxic sap). Sycamore, birch, walnut, and hickory can also be tapped for drinking water or sap to boil down for sweet syrup. This sap flows in late winter and early spring when the nights are below freezing and the days are above. Drill a hole into the tree, through the bark and into the wood.

Insert a tube to collect the water, or use a twig to guide sap to drip into a container, and then leave it there. Don't use a copper pipe or tubing, as this may harm the tree. The sap often flows best on the side of that has the most sun exposure. The sap doesn't keep long without souring, so use it within a few days. I always drink this without any need for disinfection, since wood is capable of filtering out everything but viruses.

VINES Grape vines can yield water throughout the spring in the northern hemisphere, as can vines in the tropics. Be sure you have a good field guide to woody plants to identify the right species. Small vines about a half inch (1 cm) in diameter can be cut a short distance aboveground and will drip water for some time. Larger vines can have a notch cut in them and will gush out water   from the cut (when the sap is running).

FRUITS Edible berries can be a water source when they are in season. Fill up a clean bandana or similar cloth with a pile of berries. Twist and squeeze the bundle over a clean container and the juice will pour in. The pulp and seeds can be spread out to dry and be eaten later, once a water source is secured. Remember that you shouldn't be eating if you have nothing to drink.

069 DRINK OR DIE

Dehydration can happen anywhere and in any scenario where drinking water is limited or you don't drink enough to meet your body's demand. Cold, wet winter weather is a prime example of a condition in which dehydration can sneak up on you. Nobody wants to drink water when they're freezing, but it's just as important to stay hydrated in the cold as it is in the heat. And you may need to give extra water to a sick person; illness can dehydrate the body through vomiting, diarrhea, and fever. The best way to prevent dehydration is to keep track of your water intake and urine output. You should be drinking more than two quarts a day, and urinating at least a quart and a half each day, every few hours, and the volume should seem "normal". Keep in mind that exertion, stress, health, weather, alcohol and caffeine consumption, and other factors can affect your hydration. Whatever the situation, make sure everyone is drinking enough to pee once in a while, and keep an eye out for these dehydration symptoms in yourself and your friends.

1 DIZZINESS AND HEADACHE Some of the first symptoms you may feel.

2 TIREDNESS AND WEAKNESS Motor skills and strength begin to decrease as dehydration sets in.

3 THIRST AND DRY MOUTH Obvious symptoms of a lack of water.

4 DECREASED URINATION Not needing to urinate for many hours, and producing only a small amount of dark yellow urine are signs that you're not getting enough to drink.

5 CONSTIPATION This takes a little longer to figure out, but it's definitely uncomfortable and a sign that your body is starting to dry up.

6 DELIRIUM OR CONFUSION The lack of water in your brain can lead to a deteriorating mental state.

7 SUNKEN EYES AND DRY SKIN When your skin starts to shrivel and your eye sockets start to get hollow (and it's not sleep deprivation), you're in serious trouble.

8 LOW BLOOD PRESSURE This can be very dangerous, especially if you have other health conditions that can be aggravated by this vulnerable state.

9 RAPID HEARTBEAT AND BREATHING Both of these (coupled with low blood pressure) mean that you are at serious risk of going into shock from dehydration. Immediate medical attention is required.

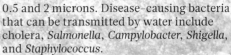

070 KNOW YOUR DANGERS

Safe drinking water can make or break an emergency situation (or your bushcraft campout). Contrary to what many survival TV shows depict, it's never wise to drink raw water from sources in the wild. Numerous pathogens can taint the water supply anywhere you go. Sure, a sip of raw water from a mountain stream may not seem that dangerous, but that mouthful of water can cause serious harm or even death, if consumed without treatment in a situation lacking medical care. Here are the things we are trying to avoid, and why we need to disinfect all raw water before drinking it.

VIRUSES The smallest of all pathogens, there are more than 100 known viruses that are transmissible to humans through drinking water. These tiny organisms range in size from 0.03 to 0.1 microns. That makes them small enough that they can even enter and infect bacteria! Waterborne viral diseases include rotavirus, enterovirus, norovirus, and hepatitis A.

BACTERIA Common organisms in surface water, pathogenic bacteria often enter waterways through dead animals in the water—and through animal and human feces—though plenty are also naturally occurring in surface water. Bacteria sizes can range between

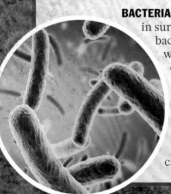

0.5 and 2 microns. Disease-causing bacteria that can be transmitted by water include cholera, *Salmonella*, *Campylobacter*, *Shigella*, and *Staphylococcus*.

PROTOZOA *Giardia* and *Cryptosporidium* are the most common forms of protozoa pathogens in raw water. They form thick-walled oocysts and cysts (shells) that allow them to survive in many conditions and even can resist strong disinfectants such as chlorine. Oocysts from . *Cryptosporidium* are small, in the range of 4 to 6 microns, while *Giardia* cysts are larger, ranging in size from 10 to 15 microns.

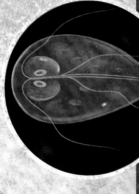

HELMINTHS In simple (and creepy) terms, these are parasitic worms found in dirty water. Depending on the species and life cycle, plenty are in groundwater. Some spend part of their lives in freshwater snails, while others can be found in water tainted with feces from an infected animal or person. Some helminths stay in your gastrointestinal tract; others migrate through the body to set up camp. Your liver, eyes, brain, lungs, and many other tender organs are at risk from these revolting creatures. The worst part is, these parasites are hard to diagnose and may lie dormant for months or even years.

071 TRY HOT ROCKS

Hot stones have been used for cooking, boiling, bed warmers, and space heaters for millennia. A stone heated to 120°F (49°C) can be the perfect hand warmer on winter campouts and hunts; and a stone heated to several times that can actually boil your drinking water and cook your food. One of my favorite bushcraft techniques is rock boiling, which can be used to disinfect water if you don't have a metal or glass container to boil in. It can also be used to prepare soups and teas, and to create steam to open up your sinuses and even heat small shelters. The upside to this technique is that you don't need any modern materials. Consider this your ultimate backup plan, should you become separated from your normal outdoor gear and find yourself thirsty for a safe drink of water.

"STONE SOUP?" Most people have heard the fable of "stone soup", but few have pondered the technology in the tale. In the story, a hungry traveler comes to a village that is running low on food. He sets up a pot of water over a fire and drops in a large rock, telling the curious villagers how delicious "stone soup" can be—but lamenting that it lacks just a few ingredients. After being tricked into providing vegetables and other ingredients, the traveler shares the finished soup with the formerly stingy townsfolk. A poor traveler might or might not have done this, for real, but maybe this traveler was just doing some hot rock cooking. Food for thought.

072 DO SOME ROCK BOILING

You can boil in a number of containers. I've used wooden and bark containers, or holes in larger rocks; I've even boiled in a hollowed-out pumpkin at Halloween (to make pumpkin and butternut squash soup), which everyone loved seeing. You can also use your Lexan plastic water bottle to boil water by the campfire. It's a great backup plan to disinfect your drinking water. Many water bottles developed for the outdoor sports industry are made from impact- and heat-resistant Lexan plastic. (You shouldn't try to put your Lexan plastic bottle over a fire to boil water in it, but you can put the heat of a fire inside the bottle using hot stones.)

STEP 1 Collect about two dozen egg-sized or slightly smaller stones to rock boil two to four quarts (or liters) of water.

STEP 2 Heat the rocks by placing them in your fire for 30 to 45 minutes.

STEP 3 Use sticks or split-wood tongs to pick up the rocks and drop them into your water.

STEP 4 If you heat up twenty or more stones in the fire, that should take care of most of your water boiling and cooking tasks.

STEP 5 Use one or two rocks at a time, rotating "cool" ones out and hot ones in.

073 DISINFECT WITH TABLETS

Iodine and chlorine are the most commonly used chemicals for purifying water and killing microorganisms. They are effective on everything when used as directed. Iodine is somewhat toxic to you over extended use; chlorine is less harmful to the body, but not always as effective as iodine, and in certain forms may not kill some protozoa like *Cryptosporidium* and *Giardia*. If you are using store bought tablets or liquids, follow the directions precisely. After mixing the chemicals and water, turn your container upside down and allow a small amount of water to run out, flushing the cap and screw threads and preventing accidental contamination. Dirty water with a lot of suspended particles and very cold water (50˚F / 10 ˚C or colder) can take longer to disinfect. It may need a stronger dose of chemicals, but be careful. You don't need a higher dose of chemicals, if you can help it. Let the muddy water settle, and let cold water warm up, if you can afford the time. Here are a few chemical cocktails that you can whip up to keep your body from becoming a tiny animal wildlife sanctuary.

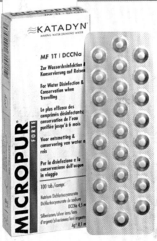

IODINE Follow the bottle directions, but this is usually 2 tablets per quart (or liter) of water. Shake the bottle a little and allow 5 minutes for them to dissolve. Turn the water bottle upside down to flush the threads and cap. Screw the cap back on tight, and wait 30 more minutes before drinking. Since they expire, get a fresh bottle of iodine tablets once a year.

CHLORINE Firstly, always follow the package directions. Usually, the tablets are sealed in foil. Remove one and drop it into one quart (or liter) of water. Shake the bottle a few times and allow 1 minute for the tablet to dissolve. Turn the water bottle upside down to flush the threads and cap, then tighten the cap again. Allow 4 hours of reaction time in a dark bottle, or place a clear bottle in a dark place. These tablets produce chlorine dioxide, which will kill everything. Micropur MP1 tablets from Katadyn are my top choice for water disinfection during a survival situation, despite the 4-hour wait time. Get a fresh package of tablets for your supplies before the printed expiration date on the package.

074 BUY THE RIGHT FILTER

You get what you pay for, but what do you really need when it comes to filtering water?

The two main types of water filters in use today are pump-action filters and drip/suction filters. The former are piston- or lever-action pumps which force raw water through a filter cartridge. The latter are filter cartridges with a gravity-drip action (like an IV bag) or they are placed in-line on hydration bladder hoses. When used on a hydration bladder, the user simply sucks water through the filter as needed. My favorite (for years now) is the Katadyn Pocket Filter. It has a ceramic cartridge with silver particles imbedded inside. The ceramic filters out the larger pathogens, and the silver kills or disables smaller organisms like viruses. Most filters like this will pump about a quart per minute. If time isn't an issue, you can opt for a gravity-fed system.

One of the smallest pieces of water-disinfecting outdoor gear to hit the marketplace lately is the "survival straw" style of water filter. Newer models can be used as a drinking-straw-type filter, and can also connect to a hydration bladder to create a gravity-drip filter. Don't expect it to filter out viruses or every single bacterium that could be in the water. But most of these filters contain an activated carbon-filter element, which effectively filters out almost all bacteria and all larger pathogens, while removing odd flavors and odors from the water.

075 DIG A GYPSY WELL

If you have source of surface water that is muddy or stagnant, this simple filtration technique won't remove all of the contaminants, but it can remove larger particles from the water, make it look and taste better, and allow most disinfection techniques to work better as well.

STEP 1 Dig a hole about one foot away from the edge of the questionable water source, using whatever means you can—even your hands. Dig the hole about one foot (30 cm) down and at least one foot (30 cm) across to make the well's volume worth the trouble. This well can be dug in dry areas also, such as dry creek beds, to allow subsurface water to collect in the hole for emergency drinking water.

STEP 2 Now, you simply play the waiting game. The hole will fill with water, as the fluid seeps through the soil. Allow the water to sit for a few hours, or overnight, to clear out some of the mud and particulates. This type of percolation well works best in sandy, silty, or loamy soils—mud and clay don't percolate very effectively.

STEP 3 Collect the water and disinfect it with the best method you have available. You can boil the water for 10 minutes, treat it with chemicals, or run it through a proper filter if it is not too muddy.

076 TRY A TRIPOD

A tripod filter is a survival water filter typically containing grass, charcoal, and sand. It won't squirt out safe water, but is an excellent first step in your disinfection system (especially important if you have muddy water, which will hopelessly clog a commercial water filter). It can be built from a wide range of natural materials and some cloth. It's slightly portable; just dump out the contents, close up the tripod, and move it to a new location. And it does improve the clarity and taste of the water when built with effective materials. Bear in mind, though, it doesn't remove many of the pathogens. You'll need to have a fire to get charcoal, or get lucky by finding remnants of someone else's fire. Depending on your location and the season, you may not find sand or green grass. It can lull people into a false sense of security regarding their water's safety.

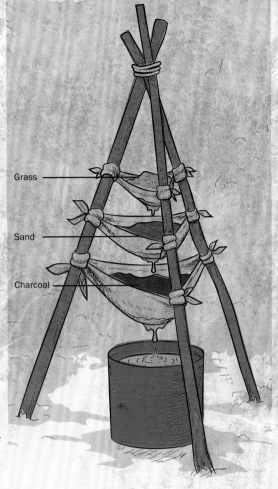

Grass

Sand

Charcoal

STEP 1 Start by collecting three sticks (live or dead) each about four and a half feet (1.5 m) long. Carve a point on one end of each one, so that the tripod legs can stick into the ground for stability.

STEP 2 Lash them together at the unsharpened end, and stand up the tripod.

STEP 3 Tie three pieces of triangular cloth into the tripod, so that each piece of cloth sits flat, one above the other.

STEP 4 Pack green grass leaves into the smallest piece of cloth at the top (if grass is not available, use a folded bunch of cloth in this layer).

STEP 5 In the second layer, add clean sand. (You can also place a thin flat stone atop each layer of your filter. This will divert the water flow and utilize more of the volume of the filter materials, rather than letting the water pour through the center of each layer unobstructed.)

STEP 6 In the bottom layer, add crushed black charcoal from a fire. Use tiny chunks of charcoal (since powder will clog up your cloth) and don't put white or gray wood ashes in the filter. (You don't want to make lye).

STEP 7 Flush out the filter by pouring water into the top level. This will remove mud and clay from your sand, and flush out tiny particles of charcoal. Once the water looks clear, place your container under the filter and pour a trickle of water into the top level of this simple gravity-fed system. This filter may remove many different particles and some of the largest organisms, but the water needs boiling, chemical or UV treatment, or maybe even filtration through a proper store-bought water filter—and that filter will now last a whole lot longer, thanks to your tripod pre-filter.

SIGNALING

You may never need to use a distress signal during your outdoor trips, and that's a good thing. But would you know how to call for help if things took an unexpected turn for the worse? Signaling is a little-practiced skill set that's truly one of the unsung heroes of the survival game. It's the skill that gets you rescued!

077 PICK THE RIGHT PATH

You've found yourself in trouble in the great outdoors. Start signaling as soon as you realize you're in trouble, with as many methods as you can muster (while still allowing time for shelter, water, fire, and food procurement). Keep signaling as you work on tasks that better your situation, and until you've encountered a helpful party. But how exactly is all this done? There are three main groups of emergency signal methods: audible, visual, and electronic. The first two groups include many different items and techniques. And I'd like to think that most of us would be carrying some kind of electronic signal equipment (e.g. mobile phone and flashlight), though this group could also include PLBs (personal locator beacons, essentially a satellite rescue system) and other gadgets.

078 USE SOUND TO SIGNAL

Humans make a lot of noise—and that's not always a bad thing. Sometimes making a ruckus can catch attention and get you rescued. In this case, the louder, the better.

YELL What is the first thing people start doing when they get in trouble? They yell "Help!" as loudly and as often as they can. Yell for rescuers, or to locate a lost member of your party. Just don't lose your voice; yell when it counts, and stop before you lose your ability to vocalize loudly.

WHISTLE To get attention, whistle in a pattern of repeating blasts, whether you're using a store-bought signal whistle or making do with breath and fingers. Remember that the old Morse code signal for help is SOS. Three short, three long, and three short sounds make up the signal. Do it at regular intervals to maximize your chances of getting noticed.

STRIKE Beat on pots, pans, car hoods, or anything else that makes some significant noise. Use hardwood sticks or clubs to strike dead trees and logs, as these can resemble the loud crack of a baseball bat. Just be loud, and use your best representation of the SOS pattern—three sets of three noises.

SHOOT Gunshots can be a very loud long-distance signal. Just fire three rounds into the dirt (not the air!) at regular intervals, if you can spare the ammo. You probably don't want to do the traditional SOS; just do three shots in a row, five seconds apart. This may not bring any help—bystanders may just think you are sighting in your rifle, or even be scared to approach a shooter. Shots at night make the most sense for signaling purposes, but save some rounds for survival hunting purposes.

CAVEMAN'S CORNER

079 KEEP IT SIMPLE

In a survival scenario where you are short on signaling supplies, one of the best tips is to use the environment as a resource, by using primitive signals.

A TRY CHARCOAL Use partially burned sticks to write messages and draw arrows on trees, rocks, and other materials. These messages can be simple words like "help" or "SOS," or more detailed messages. Arrows can also be drawn to point toward your location, in a circle around your survival camp, or even in concentric rings around your campsite. These arrows can be just the ticket to lead search and rescue personnel right to your door. These marks are long-lasting, but do not harm the trees or leave a permanent scar on the landscape.

B MAKE 3-D ARROWS In clearings and on trails, turn the charcoal arrow concept into three-dimensional reality by assembling stick and log arrows to point searchers toward your camp or trail. Set these where they will be seen, and make them obviously unnatural. Symmetrical shapes and patterns aren't usually seen in fallen limbs and logs, and if you have it, use a charcoal chunk to scribe your name and predicament on a log.

C BUILD A CAIRN A cairn is a stack or tower of rocks that is clearly man-made. These simple structures are often used in rocky treeless terrain to mark trails and provide landmarks. The same stack can be a signpost to search and rescue crews, especially if you incorporate an arrow to lead them in the right direction. Cairns can be easy to make if flat rocks are available, but even with chunky rocks you can still build this pathfinding pillar.

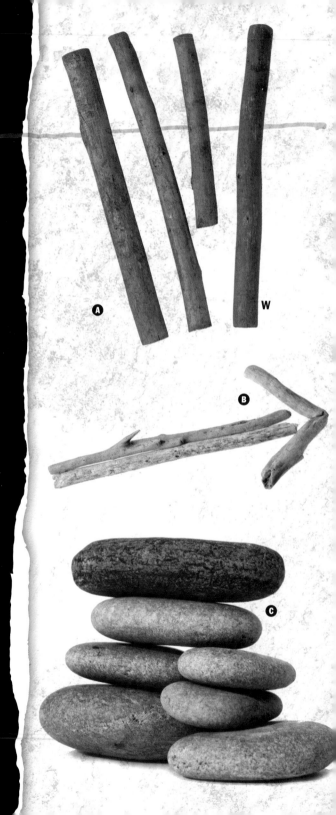

080 MIND YOUR MIRROR

A signal mirror is one of the farthest-reaching nonelectronic signal methods. Properly aimed, a signal mirror can shine a beam of daylight up to 10 miles (16 km), drawing the attention of distant aircraft, vehicles, or people.

Purchase a mirror with a sighting lens, and practice using it with a friend in a large open area. If you both have mirrors, make a game of your practice time. Try a game like "who can blind the other guy the most?" or something similar, for immediate feedback.

If you have a mirror without a sighting lens, hold the mirror under your eye, direct the beam to the tip of an outstretched finger, and then place that illuminated finger just below your target. Sweep the mirror very slowly right to left, and up and down. This should sweep the beam across your target and hopefully they will notice it. You can also use a stationary object as a "sight" to aim your beam of light.

081 HIT THE SURVIVAL STORE

There are plenty of goodies to assist in signaling. Your local outdoor store will have some, and a good hardware store will have others. Consider adding these to your survival kit or bushcraft bag. You never know when you'll need them.

WHISTLE The humble whistle is a fine piece of signal gear for short-range audible signaling. Three blasts of the whistle are generally interpreted as a universal signal for distress. Select a brightly colored whistle that will be easy to spot if dropped. It should be attached to a lanyard, ring, or clip to prevent loss. Pea-less whistles (no moving parts) are best for subfreezing weather, as your spit can freeze the little cork ball in place. Whistles are the perfect signal device to give to your kids—they're easy to operate, and most kids like making noise.

HANDHELD FLARES A flare can provide a reasonably bright light for signaling, and it also makes a great backup fire starter. To give your flare some more reach, duct tape the end of a flare to a pole or branch and wave it around. Just make sure you don't wave the flare directly overhead, in case it comes loose unexpectedly.

FLARE GUNS A staple signal method on watercraft, the flare gun can garner a lot of attention. But before you start firing off rounds, consider the danger of wildfire in your location. Many flares are still burning when they hit the ground. Dry brushy areas, arid grasslands, and dry pine forests are horrible places to use a flare gun. For safety, restrict flare guns to wetland areas and on the open water.

SURVEY TAPE A little bit of electric blue or hot pink survey tape can be a great addition to your kit. Use strips of this easy-to-tear material to make or mark trails and even leave messages. A similar product, called bird scare flash tape, is available in gardening catalogs. It's a highly reflective tape used around berry bushes and orchards to scare off scavenging birds and is also handy for catching the eyes of humans.

PERMANENT MARKER Buy and carry one of these and you now have the ability to write and make marks on virtually any dry surface. Did you get lost? A marker (plus a little survey tape) can indicate trails that you can use to prevent further wandering, and create weatherproof trails so that rescuers can better find you. Don't have the survey tape? Then write on any kind of surfaces on which the marker will show up—smooth rocks, bark-less logs, or whatever. Yes, it's graffiti, but it could also get you rescued.

082 SPARK A SIGNAL FIRE

Smoky in the day, bright at night—what's not to like? You can even boil your water and stay warm next to a signal fire. Fire is your best friend in the wild, when it does what it is supposed to. And fire can be used as a very effective signal for help, with many documented successes over the past centuries. So how can you go wrong with a giant fire? Well, let's back up. How can you go wrong with a giant fire in a place where it will not get out of control and destroy the landscape as a raging conflagration? (That's a fancy word for "hellfire.") There's a fine line of control when lighting and maintaining big fires, and you'll always need to be careful if there is any wind and any amount of dry vegetation downwind of the blaze.

STAY IN THE OPEN Fire should be in a very visible place, so that both the smoke and light are visible. If you cannot find an open place, or cannot move to that place, then you will have to rely on a thick column of smoke to do the work without the benefit of the firelight. Deep forest or jungle can really hinder signal fires, especially when the smoke is diffused through the canopy and it appears to be nothing more than mist.

CONTROL IT Keep it in a place where it won't get away from you. The middle of, say, dry grasslands on a breezy day, is a very bad place to burn a big fire. Don't let the fire get so big that you cannot put it out with the means you have at hand.

STAND OUT Unless you have a ton of black-smoking birch bark, everything else you would burn in the wild will produce a white smoke. If it is a cloudy day or foggy, no one will notice your white smoke. Throw a few ounces of motor oil, brake fluid, or any other petroleum substance into the fire to produce black smoke, which is much more noticeable.

FINISH IT OFF Put fires out cold when they have done their job. Before the rescue chopper lifts you out, or the search party escorts you away, put the fire out with water and make sure it is dead.

083 BUILD IT AND THEY WILL COME

Let's get to ground-to-air signal construction. A large "V" shape is an international signal for "we require assistance." It can resemble a naturally occurring shape, but it's easy to build with logs or other long materials. A giant "X" means "we require medical assistance" or "unable to proceed," depending on the pilot's training; it's also a less frequently seen shape in nature. Build your "X" with wood or rock, or dig the shape into soft ground. You can use string lines to make it straight, or drive a stake at each end of each line to "eyeball" for straight lines. Also, try spelling out "SOS" or "HELP." .

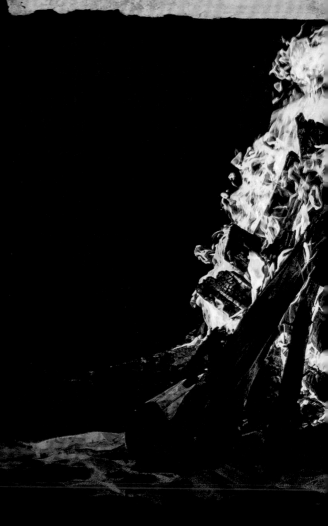

You can also throw a giant, perfect circle around your other signal shape for emphasis. If you have a lot of string or rope, like 100 feet (30 m) for example, tie one end of the cord to a stake in the ground in the center of your signal. Then walk around the perimeter with the free end of the cord, making scuff marks as you go. Once you have marked out the perimeter of your 200-foot (60-m) diameter circle, outline it with rocks, logs, or whatever to create your visible perfect circle. You can always add other signals to the classic ground to air signal, like a smoky fire and/or reflective items. Build the greatest show on earth and you'll get a free ticket home.

084 GET NOTICED

At last, pop culture can do you some good. I'm sure you have seen some show or even a cartoon involving a big SOS on the ground or the word "HELP" spelled out in giant letters. Those are actually effective signaling techniques, with a proven track record of saving lives. Ground-to-air signals that are made in the field can certainly work. But you'll need to focus on a few basic rules to give yourself the best chance of getting noticed.

GET ON OPEN GROUND A signal under the trees will not help you. Get to open ground, preferably high ground. Find a clearing, go to the beach above the tide line, get to a place where your hard work of signal building may pay off.

MAKE IT BIG I'm talking about "crop circle" big. If it's not dozens of yards (meters) across, you're kidding yourself. You want to be able to catch the attention of people who are looking for you, and even people who are not looking for you.

GET HIGH CONTRAST If you are on snow or light-colored sand, go with a dark signal material like evergreen boughs, burned logs, dark rocks, or anything that you can color with charcoal. If you are in a dark area, build with brighter colored things like pale-colored bark, sun-bleached logs, or color things yourself with white wood ashes, clay dust, or mud that dries with an ashy, pale color. If you could find some ochre stones, you could grind them into a powder and add a little water to make a red, orange, or yellow paint. Warning: Don't make a paste of wet wood ashes to paint anything. The wood ash and water combination becomes caustic and will give you a chemical burn on your skin.

MAKE IT ARTIFICIAL If there is a long line of driftwood on the beach, don't let your signal get mixed up in it. Log jams, rock outcroppings, and many other natural occurrences can resemble a ground-to-air signal, or cause your signal to blend into the landscape. Make sure yours is clearly not a natural pattern or formation.

085 FIND A WAY

First things first: Everybody should travel the backcountry with a map and compass, and some kind of electronic navigation. Even if it's just an app on your phone, GPS navigation can help find roads, waterways, ranger stations, and towns. If your tech goes down, you still have map and compass as a backup. But let's say you lose all those things somehow—now you have to navigate by memory or logic. Ideally, you've studied the map of your chosen recreational area until you could draw it from memory, but few people go that far. Even if you remember something simple, like a road to the east, you can use the rising and setting sun for bearings, and eventually make your way to that road.

FIND A WATERWAY If you can't remember where anything is, or you've survived a plane crash or some other event that has dropped you in unknown territory, then use natural features as navigational aids. Follow a waterway downstream. Follow a valley as it descends. Use a landmark or handrail to avoid going in circles (a real thing). In the old days, rivers were the highways through the wild and, even today, there is ample human activity near rivers. This also keeps you near a water source, which is vital for your survival.

DO NOT WAIT In 1971, a young woman (and eleven other people) survived a plane crash in the Amazon. The thick jungle vegetation cushioned the fall, but swallowed the plane wreckage and stymied any search efforts. Separated during the crash, she was unaware that others had survived. This ill-fated group decided to wait for rescue, while the girl set out on her own following a river. Ill-equipped and largely unskilled, she at least knew that people lived along the waterways. After more than a week, she found a small cabin and encountered hunters who escorted her back to civilization. Even with the girl's explanation of the crash site, it took searchers weeks to find it and, during that time, the other survivors perished. The moral of the story is simple: If you don't think anyone will be able to find you easily, go find them while you have the energy.

086 ASSESS YOUR RESCUE OPTIONS

You're lost in the wild. Time to determine if self-rescue is a good idea or if you will be in more danger. Normally, you'd stay put in a survival scenario, maybe light a big fire in a prominent place, and wait for help to arrive. Other situations demand another approach. Ponder these factors—and pray you never have to mull this over for real.

CAN YOU TRAVEL? If you have been injured in the wilderness and cannot move, stay put, and signal for help as best you can! But if you are at least somewhat mobile, choices lie open to you.

DOES ANYONE KNOW WHERE YOU ARE? If you've told someone where you are going and when

you'll return, you can expect help if you are overdue. Make a camp, signal for help, and wait. But if no one knows where you are, any help you get is dumb luck. If no one knows where you are, and you can move, you need to self-rescue while you still have strength. If someone knew where you were, but help still doesn't arrive in a week, it's time to self-rescue. One week is usually the period that the largest number of personnel are searching for a survivor. After that, less people are looking (and typically, they are looking for a body). If a week has passed, then it's time to get moving. Leave ample signals in your camp that establish your identity and which direction you are headed to look for help.

ASSESSMENT CHART

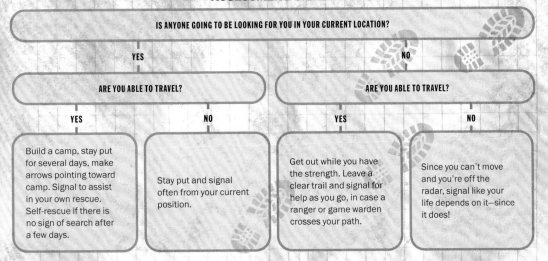

IS ANYONE GOING TO BE LOOKING FOR YOU IN YOUR CURRENT LOCATION?

YES — **ARE YOU ABLE TO TRAVEL?**

YES: Build a camp, stay put for several days, make arrows pointing toward camp. Signal to assist in your own rescue. Self-rescue if there is no sign of search after a few days.

NO: Stay put and signal often from your current position.

NO — **ARE YOU ABLE TO TRAVEL?**

YES: Get out while you have the strength. Leave a clear trail and signal for help as you go, in case a ranger or game warden crosses your path.

NO: Since you can't move and you're off the radar, signal like your life depends on it—since it does!

087 GO WITH THE FLOW

Humans are hard to track. Sometimes, they follow the path of least resistance. Search and rescue teams often find lost hikers heading downhill and following water. It's easier to hike down than up, and even the most clueless people recognize the need for a water source. SAR teams are also aware that people may ascend to a high place in hopes of getting a signal for their mobile phone or getting their

bearings for navigation. Here's my rule for self-rescue: Save your calories, walk downhill, and follow water because it'll lead you out. This works in most places on earth, with the exception of very dry climates such as deserts. In those settings, a waterway may dry up as it flows through the thirsty landscape, ending in a fan-shaped series of muddy streaks. Then you have nothing to follow and no water to drink.

FINER
THINGS

I hope you brought your appetite. In this chapter, we'll explore hunting and gathering—two ever-popular elements of outdoor survival, and for good reason. The skills you'll learn here should help you find food in almost any location. Few things provide comfort in the wilderness like a hot and tasty meal, and this section will not only show you have to make a fire in many different ways, but how to find the food to cook over that fire. By adding these abilities to your foundational skills of shelter and water, you'll change your expected survival time from a few days or weeks, to months or much longer. And if your luck holds out, you'll never go hungry again.

FIRE

If you haven't worked with fire very much, it's hard to express the emotional connection many of us feel with it—but the benefits are easy to understand. Fire gives us light in the darkness and warmth in the cold. It boils our water and cooks our food. It scares away imaginary fears and very real predators. In short, fire is one of our most valuable tools in the wilderness, and a source of many creature comforts.

088 PICK A SAFE FIRE SITE

Before you kindle your fire, pick the right location, both to make the most of the fire's heat and light and for safety.

STEP AWAY Build your fire at a safe distance from any shelter, be it a hut, tent, lean-to, or shanty, a minimum of 3 yards (3 m). Take three big paces away from your shelter in the direction of the prevailing winds. Tiny sparks can easily ignite natural shelters and burn holes in tents or tarps. Also look for an area with plenty of natural wind blocks, to keep the wind from blowing sparks.

DON'T BE A CAVEMAN Don't even try to build your fire under a rock overhang or in a cave. The heat could cause the rock to expand, crack, and collapse on you.

WATCH THOSE TREES Don't build a fire under any trees. Dead evergreen branches and needles are a major fire hazard. If there is snow on limbs above the fire, it will likely melt and fall directly on the fire.

PREVENT WILDFIRES Pick a spot clear of debris and leaves, or clear the ground of flammable materials at least 1 yard (1 m) away from the fire in all directions. It also pays to dig down into the soil to check for dry materials, which can start wildfires. Finally, don't build fires next to any dead stumps, fallen logs, or standing dead trees. The rotten wood may smolder for days and start a fire later.

089 RESPECT THE FIRE

I love campfires. Finding materials, preparing wood, and lighting a fire in a safe, traditional manner are all special to me. I hope you'll come to feel the same way, but know a couple of things. Firstly, if you're not careful, fire can turn the most important things in your life into heaps of ash. Never play with it.

And once you get a taste of fire building, you may want to make fire all of the time. People may think you're a little weird, but you may find yourself thinking about fire as much as they think about shopping or the superiority of their regional sports team. Fire will get in your blood, and you'll be glad that it's there.

090 GATHER YOUR TINDER

Tinder, the first fuel your spark falls on, is the foundation of any fire. We'll learn how to use it properly in the pages that follow but first, let's look at the wealth of options available.

① WOOD SHAVINGS This tinder comes right from firewood and may be the driest option available in wet areas, since the inside of standing dead wood is usually dry under the bark, below the wood surface. Fine shavings can be scraped from most dead, dry branches (or even bamboo) with a knife, or some kind of scraper. The wood must be dead and dry in order to scrape and burn properly. Scrape away from yourself, catching the shavings in a container. These can often be used as your sole tinder, packed tightly into a bird's-nest shape. If the shavings are too small to hold together, you can use them as the core of a bundle made from a rougher tinder, or mix them throughout the outer bundle. This is the most labor-intensive tinder to make, but if there is firewood to burn, you have tinder to light it.

② PINE NEEDLES The dead needles from most pines and similar evergreens can be used as tinder. Pine needles handle dampness very well, perhaps better than any other tinder. Because of the small amount of flammable pitch in the needles, they should burn well unless wet or rotten. Pine needles usually need no processing, but some pounding will split and shred them.

③ WEED TOPS AND SEED DOWN The dead tops from many plants can be useful here. Indeed some have several grades of tinder in their dead flower heads. Goldenrod, for example, has a fine down that is surrounded by a papery chaff on slender twigs. These mixed grades of tinder can burn well, and they serve as a great example of the way we should blend different grades of tinder. Seed down can be used as a tinder, although it usually just smolders, but can also be used as a coal extender or turned into char cloth. The down from thistle, cattail, milkweed, and even a few trees, like cottonwood, can be used. Weed tops usually need no processing. Seed down may need to be removed from pods, fluffed, and shaken to remove seeds. It is a good idea to drop or plant the seeds to renew the

5 **LEAVES** Most dead leaves make for good tinder. Their tolerance to dampness varies among types of leaves and levels of decay, but dead leaves are usually somewhat resistant to dampness. They're best when they have been harvested away from the ground, as they will be drier. Frequently, twigs with dead leaves still attached to them can be found hanging on branches and shrubs in the woods. Many oak and beech trees hold on to some of their leaves through the winter. When it is raining, look under leaning tree trunks, rock overhangs, in hollows at the bases of trees, in the dry centers of brush and leaf piles, under evergreen trees, and any other sheltered spots to find dry leaves. Crumbling is the main process to turn dead leaves into usable tinder. If dead leaves don't crumble, they may be too moist or too green to burn well. Leaves can be crumbled to make a core in many other types of tinder or used alone. For the latter, crumble some leaves to make a core of fine material and then use whole leaves for a wrapping (see item 091).

6 **INNER AND OUTER BARK** The dead inner bark from tulip poplar, cedar, juniper, mulberry, some oaks, and other woods can be processed into great tinder. Some outer bark materials can also be used such as cedar, juniper, and finely shredded paper birch. Plants that are prized for cordage material, such as milkweed, dogbane, and fireweed can also be used to provide inner bark tinder. Inner bark can be processed by methods including pounding, tearing, twisting, scraping, or buffing. The fibrous outer bark can also be processed in the same way. Pounding is usually the best way to fluff up almost any bark but that of the birch, which should be shredded as finely as possible. When processing in any of the ways listed above, catch the fine fibers that fall out during processing and use them as the central core of the finished bundle. Bark fiber can be coiled around to form a bird's nest–shaped tinder bundle. This is easily done by hand, and the finer materials should be placed in the center to provide the best fuel for the coal. These inner barks can be among the longest-burning and steadiest-burning tinder. They are good for most, if not all, conditions.

resource. Weed tops can be mixed together into bird's nest-shaped bundles, with the finer material in the center. There may need to be some outer layer to hold loose materials together. Seed down can be mixed with any tinder bundle for up to one quarter of its volume, or used as an inner core.

4 **GRASSES** Most species of grass yield good results used alone or mixed with other materials, especially in dry conditions. You can use leaf blades, seed tops, stems, and stalks. The grass must be dry and needs to have died on its own; live grass that's cut and dried retains nitrogen and moisture, both of which are natural flame retardants. Grass can be easily coiled into a nest, or used in a linear bundle like a torch. Any finer materials should be placed in the center of either bundle type to provide the best fuel for embers and char cloth. Grass may not light or stay lit if damp, and if very dry, it can burn so fast that it doesn't have time to light kindling. Don't let any of these problems discourage you from using grass. It's abundant and it usually needs no processing to be used. Just remember that it's typically your worst choice in wet weather.

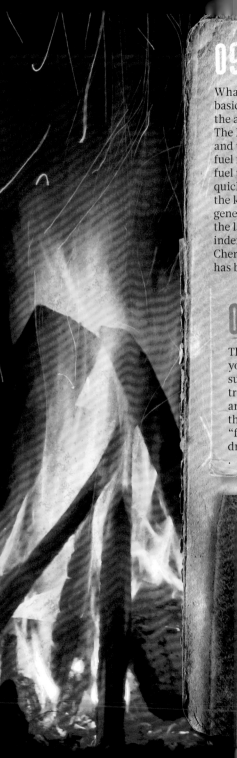

091 LEARN THE FORMULA

What's the secret recipe for bringing fire to life? You need three basic ingredients: oxygen, heat, and fuel. Oxygen is abundant in the air we breathe, so that leaves us responsible for the other two. The heat comes from our ignition source (like a match or friction), and the fuel comes from our surroundings. In the outdoors, our fuel needs to be dry plant material, and must be staged. The first fuel that the fledgling fire will eat is the tinder, which will burn quickly, generating the heat that will ignite the next fuel, which is the kindling. Usually dead twigs or wood shavings, kindling generates embers, igniting our third stage of fuel, firewood. Once the larger firewood pieces are burning, the fire can continue indefinitely as long as it is fed more firewood. According to many Cherokee people, a sacred fire exists today in their homeland that has burned continuously for over a thousand years!

092 GO GLOBAL

The six main tinder types described in item 090 may be the only ones you ever use, but there are many more choices across the world. In subtropical and tropical areas, the fabric-like bark of certain palm trees can make excellent tinder when ripped apart or simply folded around an ember. Some coconut shells also have fiber in their husks that make suitable tinder, and the dried husks can be used as "firewood" where fuel is scarce. In colder climates, some dead and dry mosses and ferns can be used alone or mixed with other materials.

093 KNOW WHAT NOT TO BURN

Not every flammable plant in the wild is safe to use for your fire. Black locust inner bark is toxic and can cause a headache when burned. Large poison ivy vines bear a fuzzy brown fiber, but even handling the fuzz can cause a rash. Burning the leaves of poison ivy, poison sumac, or poison oak is even more risky. The smoke can carry toxic oils which may coat your skin and clothing, or be inhaled into your lungs.

Animal-based materials such as hair, feathers, wool, leather, and fur always seem to show up as fire-starting staples in survival movies and shows. The fact is, unless they're both greasy and bone-dry, they won't stay lit.

094 KNOW THE 3 RULES OF TINDER

We've looked at a wide range of plant-based materials that you might use as tinder, and in the items that follow we'll go step by step through how those wood shavings, leaves, pine needles, and other combustibles become the foundation of your life-sustaining fire. In each case, the goal is to turn a coal, ember, or spark into a flame. Whatever material you choose, it should have these three crucial characteristics.

DEAD First, it should all be dead, but usually not rotten, plant-based materials. Decomposing plants almost always tend to lose more and more of their fuel value.

DRY The tinder should also be as dry as possible. In wet weather this may mean finding a few scraps at a time, and keeping it dry while you search for more.

LIGHT Last, it should be light and airy, and have a lot of surface area for its mass. In other words, it needs to be fluffy. Denser materials should be processed somehow to increase their surface area to reach their combustion temperature as quickly as possible.

095 PICK THE PERFECT PROCESS

Not every tinder type is ready to use when you find it in nature. It may be too coarse, too flat, or too solid to burn effectively. The right processing technique can make all the difference, giving you tinder that will burn quickly and easily. Here are some of the basics.

SHRED IT Start by tearing up large sections, and then tear it to shreds. This technique works well for tree-bark fiber (like tulip poplar, basswood, cedar, and many others). You can also shred weed tops and seed down into a fluffier form.

POUND AWAY Beating your tinder with a rock can separate the fibers nicely. Wad the fibers into a ball or fold them into a bundle, and pound them with a rock or other hard object. Pound it on a hard log or a stone for best results, turning it frequently to be sure you don't miss as spot. Keep

working until your tinder has the desired fluffiness. If you don't have a dry place to work, shred the tinder instead of pounding.

SCRAPE AND SCRATCH When dealing with trees with fibrous outer bark (like cedar, cypress, and juniper), use a knife or even a sharp stone to scrape off fibrous tinder. This can even be done on live trees without harm. You can also scrape wood to make shavings, if no other tinder is available (or dry).

CRUMPLE AND CRUMBLE Dead leaves, mosses and ferns, and many other prime tinder materials are improved with just a little crumbling. If the resulting confetti won't stick together, use a coarser tinder on the outside of the bundle to hold your material together before lighting.

096 BUILD A BIRD'S NEST

When you're lighting fires with matches or lighters, you can ball up a fistful of tinder into a round bundle and use it just like that. But a little more care needs to be taken when you are preparing tinder for a friction fire or flint and steel. A bird's nest–shaped tinder bundle is often the best choice for these ignition methods, and is quite easy to make with any fibrous materials.

STEP 1 Use your coarsest fibers first, coiling them into a circle to form the outermost layer of the bundle. Next, add some finer materials to the center, mashing them down so they resemble the cavity in a real bird's nest. Finish off the tinder nest by adding very fine fibers to the center of the nest, as a place to set your coal or char cloth.

STEP 2 Place your ember or char cloth in the center, and then carefully fold the bird's nest closed. This completely surrounds the ember with tinder; just make sure that you don't compact your bundle too tightly. This may crush and kill the ember.

STEP 3 Once the bundle is folded shut, blow through the tinder with tight lips (as if you were whistling). Find the spot that makes the most smoke, and focus your blowing there. You can hold the bundle in your hand, or place it on the ground if you're concerned about getting burned. Then be ready to place the flaming tinder into your waiting fire lay, once the fire erupts.

097 FOLD A TINDER TACO

It's not exactly easy to manipulate flat, crumbly leaves into a nest shape, but there may be times when dry leaves are your best tinder option. There's a solution: Just find a very large dead leaf, crumble a small mound of additional dead leaves on top of the big leaf, and add your ember. Fold the big leaf in half (so it resembles a taco), and start blowing into the openings of the taco (to onlookers, it will look like you are getting ready to take a bite). Blow in one end, or into the open top—whichever spot makes the most smoke. Stick with that spot, blowing gently on it until flames emerge, or a hole burns through the side. If a hole forms in the side, blow into the opening and your flames will be just a few breaths away. And seriously, who doesn't like tacos?

098 GIVE TINDER SUPER POWERS

For wet-weather fire starting, we need every advantage we can find. These challenging conditions led me to make a "super tinder" technique. Start with a good tinder bundle, and then dip about a quarter of its volume in grease or melted wax. Place it on the outside of the bundle, and once your ember is inside—rotate the bundle to keep the enhanced portion at the bottom of the bundle (away from the rising heat). Once your bundle is burning, turn it upside down so that the fuel-infused tinder is in the path of the flames. This will begin to burn at triple the burn time on your bundle—which may just give you what you need to light damp kindling.

099 GET THE RIGHT KINDLING

Kindling is the material that feeds the flames of tinder and gives your fire enough heat to burn larger pieces of firewood. Kindling can be obtained from a wide variety of sources, but like tinder, it should have some elements in common. Kindling should be as dry as possible, and you should gather a range of different sizes, from the size of a piece of wire up to the larger twigs and branches that could almost be considered firewood. To start a fire, there should be plenty of kindling, especially the small wire-like pieces. Remember that even if you have great tinder, those starter pieces should all be packed tightly together or your fire-making attempt can fail.

100 TRY THE TWIGS

Standing dead twigs of any nontoxic tree or shrub should make good kindling. They should snap off the branch if they are dead and fairly dry, unless they are an extremely flexible fibered wood like hickory. Rotten twigs have lost much of their fuel value and will usually crumble when broken. Green twigs have too much moisture to be used as kindling and will usually bend instead of breaking, unless the wood is very brash, like tulip poplar, spicebush, etc. Harvest lots of little twigs for your fire lay; honestly, you can't have too many. If the bark easily comes off any of the kindling, remove it by peeling it off. The outer bark is typically a protective structure for trees and shrubs, and most of it is not very flammable (except that of birch or cedar bark).

101 SPLIT SOME SPLINTERS

Fallen trees and broken branches can provide excellent sources of ready-made splinter kindling. A wide variety of hard and soft woods such as oak, hickory, and even pine can break, exposing splinters that are perfect for kindling. Wearing gloves, break the splinters off carefully. Use them alone or with other kindling. Hardwood can also be carefully split with a knife or sometimes pulled apart by hand to make splinter kindling. But be careful not to get small splinters in your hands while breaking this kindling.

102 PUT DEAD VINES TO THE TORCH

The dead vines of greenbrier, honeysuckle, and many wild grape varieties can be used as good kindling. Furthermore, old honeysuckle vines have a papery outer bark that makes good tinder. And old grape vines have a rough, shaggy outer bark that can be used as a bridge between tinder and kindling. Just make certain with a field guide that you don't have poison ivy in your kindling pile, so avoid all hairy or fuzzy vines.

103 GO BARKING MAD

Paper birch and other birches have smooth outer bark that peels off horizontally around their trunk and branches. This bark can be carefully harvested with no damage to the tree, as long as it is naturally peeling away. The bark peelings have a high content of volatile oils which, once ignited, will burn furiously even when damp. This bark can be placed throughout other kindling materials to help in any fire-making effort, particularly in wet weather.

104 MAKE THE PERFECT FIRE LAY

A fire lay is a small structure made from sticks and tinder to facilitate the ignition of a fire, and there's no shortage of any architectural variety when building these little houses for your fire to live in. The same small pile of twigs and brush and the same matchstick can be combined in a number of different ways to start a fire. But which fire lay is the right one for your particular situation? These are a few of the most common and popular fire lay constructions, with notes as to why you'd want them, and why you might not.

TEST A TIPI The simplicity of the tipi is hard to beat. This cone of sticks has a great fuel-to-air ratio, which equals a great burning fire lay that is quick lighting and dependable—even with damp materials. Your tipi can be built one stick at a time, but that's a lot of trouble. Instead, form the cone as you collect your sticks, stuffing some tinder into the center of the cone and setting it down when you're ready to light it. This is both an efficient and effective fire lay in a wide range of conditions, with a wide variety of materials, but it can fall over, and sometimes the center burns out before the sticks on the perimeter light up.

LIGHT A LOG CABIN A thing of beauty to behold, the log cabin fire lay is the most complex fire lay, short of some of the Native American ceremonial fires that I have been honored to see firsthand. The basics of the log cabin are a square "fence" of sticks with a tinder pile in the center, or a tipi in the middle. These lays burn well enough, and they even burn longer than other fire lays. It's a dependable and long-burning fire lay, although it does have a lengthy build time, and often takes up extra material.

LEARN THE LEAN-TO The classic lean-to fire lay is quick to assemble and effective under a wide range of conditions. Grab a hunk of firewood, or better yet, a large, dry curled-up bark slab. Lay your kindling perpendicular to the log or edge of the bark. Throw some tinder underneath and light it up. It's quick to assemble, and it can be made with a frugal amount of material, but it needs to be oriented into the wind for decent results, otherwise it won't have good air flow.

SPARK A CENTER POLE Tired of your fire lay falling down on the job? Grab a thumb-wide dead stick about a foot long. Stab that stick into the ground in the center of your fire pit. Place a ring of tinder around it, and lay kindling in a ring around the central pole. The result is a very sturdy tipi shape that won't fall over. This is a very stable setup, which is good for kindling materials that are having any trouble standing up on their own, although the central post interrupts the air flow in the heart of the fire lay.

HEAP UP A HAYSTACK This is the easiest fire lay to build. Just heap some kindling pieces on top of a mound of tinder. Let the sticks fall where they may, then use your hands to loosely form the pile into a rounded mound. Quick and easy, this style of fire lay works very well with short or broken kindling bits and wood shavings. On the other hand, it's a slow burner and doesn't breathe as well as other fire lays.

105 KNOW YOUR OPTIONS

Even though matches and lighters seem like modern inventions, both have deep roots in history. In China, sulfur-tipped matches were used to start fires as far back as the year 577. And the earliest modern-type lighters date back to the 1800s, burning hydrogen or methane gas. Today's matches and lighters are must-have items that will provide you with an open flame to light even the most stubborn tinder, and every single outdoor enthusiast should be carrying them.

SAFETY MATCHES These are the most common modern matches, made from a blob of potassium chlorate (with a few other ingredients) at the end of the stick. Safety matches ignite when drawn across a striker strip (typically made from red phosphorus and powdered glass).

STRIKE ANYWHERE This type of match usually has a two-color head, and it contains all of the necessary chemicals to ignite when it's scraped against any rough, dry surface.

SURVIVAL MATCHES Often coated with a waterproof varnish, survival matches (aka lifeboat or storm matches) have more flammable chemicals on their heads and an oxidizer, and they also typically burn longer than any other matches.

BUTANE LIGHTER With the flick of your thumb, butane is released from a small cylinder in the lighter. It passes beside a spark wheel that showers sparks into the gas for ignition.

106 STRIKE A ONE-MATCH FIRE

Lighting a "one-match fire" is a great display of your technique, especially in any wet or windy weather. If you want to make sure you can pass the test, use the following techniques.

START FROM UPWIND This tactic allows the breeze to push the flames through your fire lay.

PROTECT YOUR MATCH Many one-match fires fail long before the match even gets close to the fire lay. Use your body and hands to shield the infant flame from the oncoming breeze.

STAY CLOSE Strike your match very near to the fire lay, by kneeling or sitting right next to it.

LIGHT THE FIRE LOW Since the fire likes to climb, make sure you have your match at the base of the fire lay.

GET HELP Don't be afraid to use a fire helper in cold, wet, or windy weather. Fire-starter cubes, liquid fuel, fire paste, or even some drier lint could be a lifesaver.

107 DOUBLE YOUR MATCH SUPPLY

Wouldn't it be nice to double your match supply? You can do this by splitting paper-book matches in half. Tear one free from the book, and gently start peeling it apart from the torn end. Make sure the split gives you equal paper on each side. When your split reaches the chemical head, it should pop into two pieces. These "half matches" only have half the burn time of a regular paper match, but they do still work.

108 LIGHT IT UP

While it's far from primitive, the butane lighter is a one-handed fire-starting option that is both reliable and effective. You can produce flame instantly and ignite materials that sparks cannot light. If your lighter starts acting up, try one of these tricks.

WARM THINGS UP The cold can cause butane to turn into a gel and prevent it from escaping as a gas. An easy fix for this is to carry the lighter inside your clothing to keep it warm.

SPARK A NEW FLAME If your lighter's spark wheel breaks, use a bit of duct tape to hold down the button and strike sparks near the business end of the lighter. These sparks will ignite the butane gas and create a flame.

DON'T SWEAT GETTING WET If the lighter gets wet, you only need to shake it or blow on the spark wheel to dry it out and restore function.

109 MAKE YOUR OWN WATERPROOF MATCHES

If you can't find waterproof matches at the store, then you can make them yourself. Melt a few ounces of candle wax in a shallow container (like a tuna can). Dip the match head quickly, and then blow on it to harden the wax. When it's fire time, scrape off the wax and strike it!

Flint and steel is an early fire making technique that dates back to the very first days of metal experimentation in Europe and Asia. This fire starting method creates a red hot spark by striking a piece of high carbon steel against a hard, sharp stone edge (like a flake of flint). The steel shaving is ignited by the friction of striking steel and stone together. This steel spark is immediately caught in fire charred material, then placed in dry tinder and blown into flame.

Materials

STEEL STRIKER The striker is a piece of high-carbon steel that is often worked by a blacksmith to achieve the right hardness and shape. Strikers are often made from old files, machetes' and other tools.

FLINT The "flint" can actually be almost any type of stone that is sharp and harder than the steel striker. Examples include flint, of course, along with chert, jasper, agate, granite, or quartz.

CHAR CLOTH This is some form of blackened, plant based material for catching and feeding a spark. Cotton and linen are traditional American frontier char cloth materials; however, most flammable plant fibers, tinder, some shelf fungi and punky, rotten wood can be turned into "char cloth."

Technique

Strike the stone downward across your steel, holding the stone at a 45-degree angle to make steel sparks. These sparks come from the carbon in the steel—and the sparks can be scraped off by any sharp stone that is harder than the steel. Amazingly, the metal is heated by the intense friction right at the point of the sharp stone edge. As the tiny metal shavings are removed, they become white-hot little spheres of metal. When scraped over char cloth or some other fine tinder, these minute orbs of molten metal can ignite a fire.

Some people prefer to throw sparks into a container of char material, and then scoop out any embers that have lit. I prefer to strike sparks onto char cloth that is already sitting in a bird's nest shaped bundle of tinder. Why not try them both?

Bright Sparks

Having trouble aiming your sparks? Wrap a flexible piece of char cloth around your flint edge and strike through the cloth. Some sparks are guaranteed to hit. You could also hold char under your thumb lightly, right by the stone edge as you strike. Once your char has begun to glow red, then place the burning char cloth into the tinder. Be careful of burned thumbs with either trick.

Troubleshooting

As with many skills, there is a learning curve for flint and steel. Starting out, you should wear safety goggles and leather gloves to protect your eyes from flying stone chips and your hands from cuts—unless you like scraping off more knuckle than steel. The striking edge of the flint should be 90 degrees or less, though an edge less than 45 degrees will work best.

Just remember that practice makes perfect.

IF YOU ARE HAVING TROUBLE STRIKING SPARKS:
- change the angle of the flint
- use a sharper edge on the flint
- strike harder or possibly softer with the striker
- change your striking motion

IF THE SPARKS WILL NOT CATCH ON THE CHAR CLOTH:
- strike the sparks closer to the char cloth
- change the angle at which you are striking sparks
- change out the char cloth with a different material

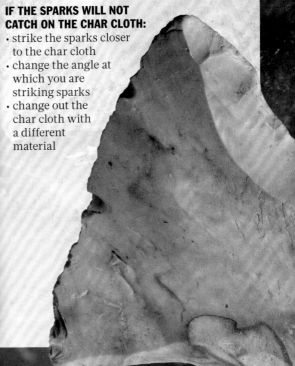

111 SPIN A BOW DRILL

The bow and drill is an ancient method of fire making in which a wooden drill is rotated back and forth on a wooden board. A small bow is used to cause this reciprocating action, and the drill is topped with a handhold block to offer stability and downward pressure. As the drill spins against the fireboard, it generates dust and heat. When the dust gets hot enough, it forms an ember that you can kindle into flame.

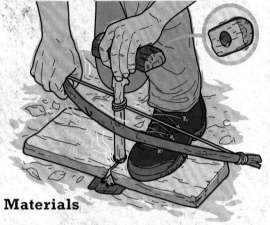

Materials

BOW The bow should be a flexible limb about 2 feet (0.6 m) long and as thick as your thumb. Use a thick cord or a thin rope for the bow string.

DRILL The drill should be a smooth cylinder of soft dry wood, about thumb thickness and 10 inches (25 cm) in length.

FIREBOARD Use a flat board of softwood to receive the drill. The fireboard should have a hole for the drill with a notch carved in it to let the dust out.

HANDHOLD This is a piece of hardwood, bone, or stone with a hole in it, which should be lubricated with a greasy or waxy material before drilling.

> **PRO TIP** Many things can be used as handhold lubricant. Animal fat, oily nuts, pine pitch, fatty insects, crushed evergreen needles, or even a glob of ear wax will work! Just place the material in the handhold and grind it with the top of your drill to release the oil or wax.

Technique

STEP 1 Carve a point on each end of your drill and then carve a pilot hole in the top of the fireboard. Tie the cord onto your bow, and lubricate your handhold.

STEP 2 Wrap the bow string tightly around your drill. Pin the drill between the handhold and the fireboard pilot hole. Then begin the drilling to burn in a hole.

STEP 3 Once the hole has been burned in, carve a notch in the side of your board to collect the dust. The notch should be a 45-degree wedge, just shy of the center.

STEP 4 Start drilling slowly, then speed up while pushing down hard on the handhold. The notch in the fireboard should begin to fill with dark brown dust as smoke wafts out. Keep drilling until the notch is overflowing, then drill faster to light the dust. No flames will appear, but the dust pile will continue smoking if you made an ember. Drop this newly formed ember into your tinder, and blow it into flame.

Troubleshooting

There are a lot of things that can go wrong with a bow drill; these tips may make things easier.

- If you have trouble turning the drill or getting brown dust, choose a more slender drill.

- If the coal goes out before being wrapped in the tinder bundle, try again and drill beyond the point where you think you have a coal.

- If the cord slips around the drill, tighten the cord, or back off on the downward pressure.

- If the cord rides up and down the drill, take longer, more level strokes with the bow. The bow should be parallel to the ground and in the middle of the drill.

- If the handhold smokes or heats up, apply more lubricant.

- Keep the drill and fireboard dry as possible.

112 USE A HAND DRILL

Similar in operation to the bow and drill method, the hand drill is a primordial friction fire method that creates an ember when you twirl a slender drill against a wooden board with your bare hands. Since there's no bow or handhold, this method is much harder than the bow drill, but here's the advantage; It only takes four items to get your fire (the drill, board, tinder, and a knife). When you're ready for a challenge, give the hand drill a try.

Materials

DRILL The drill for this method is typically a dead, dry weed stalk about 20 to 30 inches (50 to 75 cm) tall. Mullein, yucca, velvet leaf, horseweed, and goldenrod are great choices, all commonly available.

FIREBOARD The hand–drill fireboard is a small thin board, typically the same thickness as your drill. Softwood species are best, and your board will need a hole for the drill and a notch carved in the side just like the bow drill. Willow and basswood are excellent board choices.

COAL CATCHER This is a flat chip of wood, bark, or bone, or a dead, dry leaf under the notch in the fireboard to catch the coal and allow it to be transferred to the tinder.

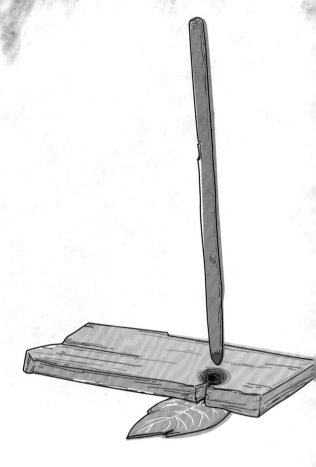

Technique

STEP 1 Select a dead weed stalk for your drill and sand away any rough spots.

STEP 2 Carve a piece of wood flat and drill a pilot hole in the top. Spin the drill to burn into the board, then carve a notch into the edge.

STEP 3 Spit on your hands or apply a little pine pitch to the drill for grip. Spin the drill quickly while pushing downward. When you reach the bottom of the drill, quickly move back to the top and start spinning again. Drill until the notch is full of dust. If the dust doesn't form a coal, leave it in the notch and do several more speed runs for ignition.

STEP 4 When the dust is glowing or smoking, add tiny amounts of coal extender to help it grow. Be careful; a light breeze will blow it apart and a drop of sweat will extinguish it.

Practice Makes Perfect

The hand drill is one of the toughest friction fire methods, so identifying and correcting problems is critical to your success.

GO THE DISTANCE You'll really need to build up your strength, stamina, callouses, and skill to enter into the ranks of veteran hand drill fire makers. Don't give up!

KEEP IT DRY Moisture can prevent the dust from getting hot enough to form a coal, so keep your drills and fireboards as dry as possible.

MAKE A MATCH Board and drill density should be similar. If the drill burns quickly through the board, then select a harder board or use a wider drill.

FOCUS YOUR FRICTION The friction area should be at the bottom of the drill, not on the sides of the drill or up inside a hollow drill. Trim the walls of the fireboard hole to avoid any side friction, and if a bump forms in the bottom of the fire hole, carve it out.

A Little Something Extra

Hand drill coals are often small and loose; add a little coal extender over the newborn ember to make it bigger and more stable. The dust from previous attempts, shavings or dust from chaga (a hard tinder fungus growing on mountain trees), powdered rotten wood, fluffy down from plants, and other fine or dusty tinder materials can be used as coal extenders.

PRO TIP If you've got another person to help, and a handhold block, you can blend the bow drill and hand drill techniques. One person spins the drill with their hands while the other gently holds a handhold block on top of the drill to apply a little extra pressure.

113 PUSH A FIRE PLOW

The fire plow is nothing short of full-contact fire making. It's brutal, simplistic, aggressive, and exhausting. In this friction fire method, you'll rub a stick against a log until you abrade a groove into it with sheer power and strength of will. Once the groove has been made, you'll continue plowing until you pile up dust in the groove and ignite it with friction heat. This fire-making process can be done without any tools, but it's one of the hardest ways to get a flame.

Materials

PLOW STICK The plow stick should be about 20 inches (50 cm) long and about as thick as your thumb. This is the part of the kit that moves. A dead and dry yucca flower stalk is one of the greatest materials for this component, though a branch off your softwood plow log can work.

PLOW LOG Basswood, cedar, willow, or some other softwood should be used for the stationary plow log. It should be dead and dry, but not rotten. If the log has a fork at one end, this can be very helpful to keep it from rolling and to brace it up against a tree or rock. You could also use a heavy plank of similar wood.

Technique

STEP 1 Pin the log or board up against a solid object, and hold down the end closest to you with one or both of your knees. Alternately, you could have someone else hold it down by standing on the end.

STEP 2 Rub the plow stick briskly on the top of the log covering about a 10-inch (25-cm) section. The plow stick will start to abrade a groove in the top of the plow log. Rub the plow stick back and forth with great speed and downward pressure. Smoke should begin to form and dust should build up in the deepening groove.

STEP 3 The dust will be pushed to the end of the groove, and if you plow long enough and hard enough, the dust pile will begin to smolder with an ember inside. If the dust doesn't ignite, leave it in the groove and try again, or hand off to another person while you rest.

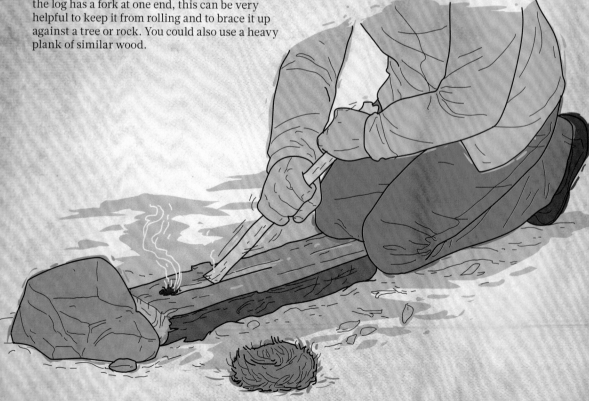

Troubleshooting

The fire plow apparatus may be the simplest to assemble, but this method needs skillful technique and brute strength to create a smoldering coal. Here are a few tricks that may get you one step closer to a fire.

- Carve a slice off each side of your plow stick to reduce side friction and direct pressure to the tip of the plow stick.

- Flip the plow stick over. Once a plow stick has been used on one side, it will develop a point on the other side. Using this sharper point can increase the pressure you are applying, due its reduced surface area.

- If you can't plow long enough, breathe harder and deeper. Since many people often hold their breath on this technique, time your breathing with each stroke so you can last longer.

Extra

Can't control your stopping point, or keep dust inside the end of the groove? Line the ground on both sides of the plow log with fluffy tinder. With luck and tenacity, you'll fling a tiny ember out of the groove and into the tinder, where you can then collect and nurse it into a flame.

PRO TIP Try to stop at the same spot at the end of your plow stroke. This will form a small shelf in the bottom of the groove, which will make it easier to stop in that spot when the plow stick hits it.

A traditional fire-starting method from the tropics, the fire saw is a very specialized technique that uses bamboo instead of tree wood. To make the technique work, one piece of bamboo is used like a saw to abrade a notch all the way through another piece of bamboo, which contains tinder. As both bamboo pieces create charred dust, this fine fuel collects in the tinder-filled section to create an ember—if you're hardworking, talented, and lucky!

Materials

SAW A 1-yard (1-m) piece of dead, dry yellow bamboo with an exposed edge that can act like a saw.

TRAY This is the piece that contains tinder and collects dust. It can be any size, as long as it's slender enough for you to hold easily, yet thick enough to be strong, even when cut nearly in half. Drill a small pilot hole through the tray for each spot you intend to saw.

TINDER AND BRIDGE These two elements hold the ember in the tray. The tinder is placed in the tray, behind the pilot hole, while the bridge is a splinter that holds the tinder in place. Hold each side of the bridge as you hold the tray in both hands.

Technique

STEP 1 With a saw or a rough stone, remove half of a section of bamboo between the two nodes. This free section will be your tray, and one of the edges on the full section of bamboo will become your saw. This "cut out" should happen on the end of the bamboo section, not in the middle.

STEP 2 Drill a small pilot hole through the tray and place tinder behind it. Use a strip of bamboo to hold the tinder in place.

STEP 3 Brace the long bamboo piece between your hip bone (padded with cloth) and the ground, supporting the long piece of bamboo against your thigh. Start moving the tray back and forth against one of the saw edges, and lined up over your pilot hole so that the dust can come through.

STEP 4 Saw briskly until you have been making strong smoke for at least 30 seconds, then check on your tinder to see if an ember has formed.

Troubleshooting

Your bamboo should be dead and dry, weathered to a nice yellow or gray color—never green. Here are some other things that will help.

- Use your knife to sharpen the edge on the saw.

- Pack tinder tightly around the back of the pilot hole, so the dust that does collect will stay in one spot, and so that your ember won't fall out.

- Carve a groove outside of your tray, right over the pilot hole, to guide the first few saw strokes.

- Don't forget to breathe! Many folks hold their breath while doing this, and they run out of energy before they can make an ember.

More Uses for Bamboo

This versatile plant can also give you the fuel to start the fire. Use your knife, axe, or a machete to split short sections of bamboo into splinters that can be used as kindling. You can even make some fluffy tinder from bamboo by scraping your knife edge at a 90-degree angle against the exterior side of a bamboo section.

PRO TIP The process described here requires a long piece of bamboo for the saw. The fire saw can also work with a smaller saw. Fill the tray with tinder, lay it on the ground, and then use a small saw piece to cut back and forth over the pilot hole.

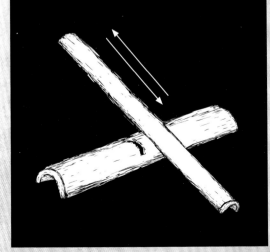

PLANTS

Foraging is the oldest bushcraft skill; human beings have been foragers far longer than we've been hunter-gatherers or farmers. Wild edible plants can't always meet your nutritional needs in every place and season, but it's still important to know what to put on your plate, to avoid poisoning yourself and to prepare your wild foods correctly. With study and careful exploration, you too can become a skilled forager.

115 COUNT YOUR CALORIES

I've said it before, and I'll say it again: Survival is all about calories. Everything we do during an emergency comes down to two actions: saving calories and getting more calories. The most basic survival requirement, then, is managing calories. Your body needs calories to function, and getting enough can be a little tricky if you're forced to rely only on the plant foods you can find in the wild.

Throughout most habitats and seasons, wild edible plants are fairly consistently a poor source of calories. Leaves, shoots, berries, tubers, and other plant parts might be filling and vitamin packed, but they all lack a high calorie count. Tree nuts are typically the only high-calorie foraged plant foods, but unfortunately these aren't always available.

Plants may play a big role in your wilderness diet, but they probably won't be able to provide the bulk of your caloric needs in the bush. That's why we always want to bring some high-calorie food from home, as well as learning how to trap, fish, and hunt.

116 SKIP THE FUNGUS

Sure, mushrooms can be delicious. And yes, it's like a treasure hunt to search for them in the wild. But are mushrooms a safe, reliable source of food for beginning foragers?

Of the world's 70,000 species of fungi, only about 250 species are considered to be a good wild food. Roughly the same number of species can kill you or put you on the list for a liver transplant. Everything else is somewhere in between these extremes. Most mushrooms and fungi are too bitter, too small, or too tough to eat—or are just toxic enough to make you wish you hadn't eaten them.

There are thousands of mushroom poisoning cases in the U.S. annually, and many, many more worldwide each year.

Remarkably, it's rare for these poisonings to be fatal, as most exposures are treatable (and happen where treatment is available), or are mild enough that no medication is required. But people can and have died, so don't risk it.

117 CHOOSE WISELY

If you've never collected your own food before, it may be thrilling or frightening (or a bit of each). Some people feel like they are taking control of their sustenance and their life for the first time, while others feel like they are taking their life in their own hands. Both are true.

GUIDE YOURSELF It's an empowering thing to harvest a meal for yourself, even if it's just a tangy wild salad or a bowl of sweet berries. But you are also taking a risk every time you forage. The devil is in the details, so pay attention to the little things. Bring reading glasses or a small magnifying loupe when you go out to harvest. Bring a field guide that contains your local edible and poisonous species, with detailed descriptions. Use that book and the information it contains to stay safe.

EAT HEALTHY The time you spend can be very rewarding, as you learn to safely harvest rare and succulent edibles. And when you're in the right place at the right time, nature's bounty is open to you. Just a little bit of work (and a lot of attention to plant details) can get you an armload of edibles. Who needs vitamin tablets when you can get a wealth of vitamins and minerals from your wild meals?

118 FORAGE SAFELY

It's important to take some basic precautions as you set out to sample local plants.

CHECK CAREFULLY The basis of plant identification is checking a plant's features against a guidebook (or your own knowledge of the species) to be sure you know what it is, and whether it's edible.

One simple piece of advice: If you even have a hint of doubt that something doesn't look quite right about a plant you are sizing up, then absolutely do not eat it.

BEWARE OF ALLERGIES Wild plants aren't there just to munch upon, and some can be very dangerous to humans. You may still have an unusual reaction to a widely tolerated plant food.

119 BE A GOOD STEWARD

It's easy to think of the great outdoors as your own personal grocery store when you first take up foraging. And in the beginning, it's very easy to over harvest—especially since everything is free. It's also easy to fixate on your own wants. If you harvested all of the edible plants in an area today, would there be more for the future?

PICK YOUR PLANTS WISELY Be a guardian to the landscape. Pay careful attention to the plants around you; your presence can benefit your local wild spaces in return. For example, when you discover an abundant delicious wild edible like garlic mustard, take all you can. This tasty weed is invasive, and can choke out native plants.

RESTOCK THE REGION You can also find out which native plants are missing from an area, and collect (or purchase) edible plant seeds to spread as you hike around. You'll have a future crop, and others can use the plants too.

120 MAKE SURE IT'S SAFE

There are plenty of things that can go wrong when you are foraging, but you can do a lot to minimize risk by following the basic rules of identifying and harvesting wild edibles.

STEP 1 Use a field guide to make 100 percent positive identification of the plant or plant part (nut, berry, flower, etc.).

STEP 2 Cross-reference your research just to make sure there aren't any dangerous look-alike species.

STEP 3 Research the right way to use the plant, which parts are safe to use, and when to use them if seasonality is a factor.

STEP 4 Learn which plants should be eaten in moderation and which will require any special preparation to eat at all.

STEP 5 Reduce the risk of allergic reaction by eating only small amounts of plants that are new to you, and try just one new food per day (after you make a 100 percent positive ID).

STEP 6 Finally, if in doubt, do not eat it!

121 KNOW YOUR NUTS

Tree nuts are a great source of calories when you're out in the wild, but you have to know which ones to look for and how to make them ready to eat.

ACORN Many native peoples in the northern hemisphere ate as a staple food prior to agriculture. These are high-carb nuts, with some fat and a little protein. The bitter acid in them is easily removed by cracking them into pieces and soaking the acorn nut meat chunks in repeating baths of warm water, 1 hour at a time, until the bitter is gone. Don't boil them—it locks in some of the bitterness.

BEECH These tree nuts can be a valuable and delicious wild food source, but you'll have to be quick, as squirrels seem to favor them above all others. Look for the smooth-barked trees in the eastern woodlands, and keep an eye out for the small three-sided seed falling out of a prickly husk around early October.

HAZELNUT There are several species of hazelnut tree in Europe, Asia, and North America. The most common tree in the U.S. is the American hazelnut, which grows east of the Mississippi from Georgia to Maine. Hazelnuts are relatively rich in calories and are also a good source of vitamin E, thiamine, copper, and manganese.

BLACK WALNUT Black walnuts look like green tennis balls on the tree, but their rough, round husks turn to a very dark brown as they lie on the ground in autumn. The nut meats are rich tasting and are high in fat, with a fair amount of protein, magnesium, phosphorus, copper, and manganese. Wild animals might even let you get some of them, primarily because they don't like to chew through those thick, bitter husks.

HICKORY The most calorie-dense wild food in our gallery, the hickory is packed with life-sustaining fat. Most varieties taste like their most famous relative, the pecan. These sweet and fatty nut meats can eaten right out of the shell or cooked in a number of ways. From porridge to cookies to a crust for your favorite game bird, hickory is an underused hero in wild foods.

CHESTNUT Part of the beech family, these deciduous hardwood trees and shrubs are found throughout temperate regions of the northern hemisphere. The nut is contained in a needle-covered cupule, also known as a "burr." These burs often grow in pairs or clusters, and each burr can hold one to seven nuts. Chestnuts are less calorie-dense, but are a good source of vitamin B6, vitamin C, and potassium.

122 PROCESS ACORNS PROPERLY

Acorns represent one of the biggest (and most widespread) calorie jackpots in the annual wild plant food harvest, They do require a bit of processing to be palatable, but they're well worth it.

STEP 1 Crack the shells, remove the nut meats, and break any large pieces into pea-sized chunks.

STEP 2 Soak the meats in warm water to remove their bitter and irritating tannic acid. Some guides instruct us to boil acorns, but this locks in some of the bitterness. Let soak for a few hours.

STEP 3 If the soaking water was safe to drink, taste a piece of acorn to see if they're still bitter. If so, drain off the water (which should be brown like tea), add fresh warm water, and soak again for a few hours. Repeat this a few times depending on the acorns' bitterness.

STEP 4 Once the acorns taste okay (in other words, bland), let them dry out for a few hours. You can run them through a grain grinder or flour mill, or use the classic mortar and pestle to make acorn flour. Add this flour to existing recipes; or try your hand at making acorn porridge, cookies, crackers, or biscuits.

123 DINE OFF A PINE

The nuts of any large pine tree are a classic Native American survival food, and an important food around the northern hemisphere. Pine nuts are more than half fat by weight, with some protein and carbs added in for good measure. They're also a good source of thiamine and manganese, with a decent array of other B vitamins and several minerals.

CRACK A CONE Generally speaking, the larger the pinecone, the bigger the seeds. And it usually takes some work to tear open a cone. Some species will open by the heat of a fire, but most won't; you'll have to tear them open with pliers or a multi-tool. But with a nutritional profile like this, and a great taste, it's worth the work.

MAKE BARK FLOUR Pine also has an edible layer to its bark. Shave off the rubbery, cream-colored inner layer of bark that's right next to the wood. Dry the strips out until they are brittle and grind them into flour. The flour will have a mild pine flavor and a fair number of calories. Extend your food supply by blending it with other flours.

124 DON'T EAT THESE

There are at least two major species you should avoid when foraging for nuts. The first is buckeye, which, like hickory, has a "double layer" nut shell—a husk that peels off with a hard nut shell underneath. Buckeyes have a shiny brown shell underneath the outer husk, while hickories have a dull tan-colored shell. Hickory has a multiple inner shell like a walnut, while buckeye has a solid meat like an almond. Also, chestnuts should not be confused with horse chestnuts, which have similar, but poisonous, nutmeat.

125 USE EVERYTHING BUT THE SQUEAL

Remember the brown, tea-like water you poured off the first soaking of acorns? Well, don't throw it out! Even though it seems like we're brewing up some kind of medieval potion, crushed acorns and hot water can provide a great remedy for inflamed and irritated skin, as well as toothaches. You can use the first water you pour off from the process of soaking acorns for food.

You can make a concentrate by boiling crushed acorns (shells and all; a handful in one pint of water will make a small batch of strong medicinal fluid). Soak a clean cloth in it, and apply to rashes, ingrown toenails, hemorrhoids, or other inflamed skin ailments. For tooth troubles, simply swish the stuff (swallowing it causes an upset stomach).

Looking to stock up on wild greens? Here are a few great examples of edible plants to pick.

CHICORY This herbaceous perennial plant, native to Europe, is found across the hemisphere. Its leaves are similar to those of the dandelion, and the stalk has smaller alternate branching leaves. The blue composite flowers have ragged square edges to the rays. Chicory may live for several years, reviving from its taproots. The leaves and flowers can be eaten, and the roots can be baked to make a coffee substitute.

CHICKWEED This herbaceous annual plant often forms a carpet on the disturbed ground of farms, gardens, and lawns. Native to Europe, it is now found in many places. The small, ovate, simple leaves grow in an opposite branching pattern on round, green stems with white flowers. The tender leaves and stems can be eaten raw (in the case of star chickweed) or cooked (if you happen to find mouse-ear chickweed). This plant can be used as a poultice for an anti-itch remedy, and can be eaten to relieve constipation.

WOOD SORREL These are common perennial herbaceous plants in the northern hemisphere, with heart-shaped leaflets in threes. Stems and leaf stalks are alternate branching, and these plants are rarely taller than 6 inches (15 cm). The flowers are yellow, pink, or purple, often with five petals. The leaves, stems, and flowers can be eaten raw in salad, or steeped in hot water, strained, sweetened, and chilled to create a lemonade substitute. Be aware: Their sour taste is caused by oxalic acid, which can lead to kidney stones. Limit yourself to occasional use.

SHEEP SORREL This small plant grows very unusual spearhead-shaped simple leaves in fields and gardens. It is a perennial herbaceous plant that has a reddish alternate branching stem, up to a height of 18 inches (0.5 m). The leaves are typically small, about 1 inch (3 cm), and smooth edged, with a pair of lobes at the base of each leaf that may point outward or down. The tender, sour leaves can be eaten raw or prepared for a drink, similar to wood sorrel. And like wood sorrel, the sour flavor comes from oxalic acid, which should be consumed in moderation to avoid the risk of kidney stones.

PLANTAIN A common weed in lawns worldwide, this annual herbaceous plant has parallel-veined, smooth-edged simple leaves that grow in a basal rosette. Torn, the leaves reveal stringy fibers inside the parallel veins, and have an astringent cabbage-like odor. The small white flowers are on slender stalks, which later grow greenish seeds. The chopped young leaves can be added to salads or boiled as cooked greens. Seeds can be eaten raw or cooked and are high in B vitamins. Plantain is also a great poultice for insect stings and venomous bites.

WATERCRESS An aquatic or semiaquatic plant native to Europe and Asia, this perennial is a relative of mustards and radishes, and one of the earliest plants consumed by humans. Watercress grows in fast, clean streams and springs, with hollow floating stems and pinnately compound leaves in an alternate pattern. The small white flowers have four petals in clusters. The leaves and tender stems have a biting, spicy flavor. Just wash them thoroughly if you decide to eat them raw, as the water they grew in could bear pathogens. Cooked watercress is not as tasty, but it is safer. Watercress is a source of vitamin C and other nutrients.

127 DIG SOME ROOTS

Some plants may not be too tasty aboveground, but their roots can be a great wild food source.

BURDOCK To prepare this root, just wash it, chop it, boil the root pieces for about 5 minutes, change the water, boil again for 5 minutes, and then taste test for flavor. (Boil again if needed, to remove the bitterness.) Burdock is a source of vitamin B6, and provides potassium, magnesium, and manganese.

CATTAIL Often labeled as the "supermarket of the swamp," this plants roots contain an edible white starch, and its shoots as well as the sprouts that grow on the roots are also edible, if low in calories. The leaves can be woven into baskets and twisted into ropes. Just watch out for iris, which is poisonous and also grows in swampy conditions. Iris is generally half the height of cattail with a large flower at the top. Cattail will be topped with a seed head that looks very much like a corn-dog in size and shape.

JERUSALEM ARTICHOKE Neither from Jerusalem, nor an artichoke, this native sunflower relative does have a slightly sweet tuber that contains lots of iron and potassium. It also provides a good dose of B vitamins. Look for the small sunflower-looking bloom in the fall at the tops of the tall plants, and dig up the tubers, which are shaped much like ginger roots.

WILD ONION Roughly a dozen different species of wild onion grow in North America. Whether closer to garlic or chives in appearance, all are part of the tasty, edible allium genus. But don't just wolf down any onion-looking plant; they are part of the lily family, which contains some toxic members. Look for the classic shapes of a bulbous root and a rounded stem of onion and garlic. Next, scratch the bulb or bruise the green tops, and you should immediately smell the familiar oniony odor. If a few tears begin welling up in your eyes, all the better; you will definitely know you have an onion or garlic genus member for sure. Use these raw or cooked, just like their store-bought relatives.

CAVEMAN'S CORNER

128 GET THE STICK

Need to dig, but lack a shovel? Do what humans have done for millennia: use a digging stick! A typical digging stick is 2 to 3 feet (0.6 to 1 m) long, and 1 to 2 inches (0.5 to 1 cm) thick, with a flat head point. Hardwood is best, as it is more durable. Use a skinnier stick in rocky soil to get between little stones and pebbles in the ground and a wider stick for loose or sandy soils. A digging stick is primarily used for loosening up soil, which can then be scooped out of the way with a flat rock, a basket, or your hands. You can use your stick to make a fire pit, dig your latrine, and perform a wide range of other survival tasks.

129 LEARN BERRIES INSIDE AND OUT

When we first learn about local berries and fruits, we often make some dangerous assumptions. For example, if most of our region's red fruits happen to be edible, it's easy to assume that all red fruits are safe to eat. Unfortunately, this thinking can get foragers into serious trouble. Skin color alone is not a safe way to judge edibility or safety. You'll need to positively determine the plant's genus and species by studying the plant's leaf patterns, branch patterns, and the innards of the fruit or berry. Before you take the first bite, check each of these seven features of fruits and berries.

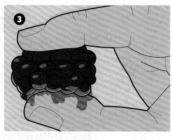

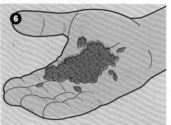

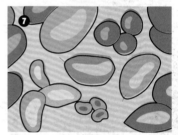

❶ EXTERIOR COLOR The color of a fruit or berry is the first thing that catches our eye and it is an important factor in identification. But it can't be your only identifier.

❷ INTERIOR COLOR This can be a key difference between berries that look the same on the outside. Check carefully against your identification guide.

❸ TEXTURE You may find pulp, pith, or juice when you squish open a fruit or berry. All of these are fine—provided they match what you're expecting to find.

❹ SEED COLOR From pale tan to jet black, the seed color inside the fruit should be the right one for that particular species.

❺ NUMBER OF SEEDS Check the seed number from several specimens and come up with an average. Some species have only one seed within, while others have many. In some cases, the difference between one and two seeds can mean the difference between an edible fruit and a very similar poisonous species.

❻ SEED SIZE Check the seed size against your identification guide to make sure you have the right fruit or berry; this is an important identifier.

❼ SEED SHAPE Seeds may be round, pointy, oblong, curved, flat, or any number of shapes. As with the other factors here, check closely to make a positive identification.

BROWSE NATURE'S GROCERY STORE

The wild holds a veritable cornucopia of edible fruits, berries, nuts, and more. Take a look at this chart to find out a little about each of the many offerings you can find in the wild that can provide a good amount of calories to your diet.

ACORNS

Calories 475 calories per each cup (125 g)
Nutrients Contains vitamin B6, folate, copper, and manganese
Where Woodland and temperate habitats throughout the northern hemisphere
When Autumn, with nuts sometimes wintering over into spring
Tips Remove the shells and soak in water to remove tannic acid

WILD STRAWBERRY

Calories 45 calories per cup (200 g)
Nutrients One cup of berries will give you more than a full day's supply of vitamin C
Where Woodland areas in North America
When A very short season in late spring
Tips Don't be confused by the Indian strawberry, which is still edible, but completely flavorless

CRANBERRY

Calories 46 calories per cup (100 g)
Nutrients One cup contains one fifth of your daily requirement of vitamin C
Where Acidic bogs and wetland areas in northern latitudes
When Berries ripen to red in autumn
Tips Eating the berries is a widely used remedy to treat and prevent urinary tract infections

BLACKBERRY

Calories 62 calories per cup (100 g)
Nutrients A cup has 50% of your daily vitamin C and 36% of your vitamin K
Where Open ground and woodland edges, throughout the northern hemisphere
When Early to the middle of summer
Tips Blackberry leaves can be dried and steeped as a tea that has a mild taste and helps treat diarrhea

BLACK WALNUT

Calories 760 calories per cup (125 g)
Nutrients Significant amounts of magnesium, phosphorus, and copper
Where Old fields and forests in the eastern half of North America
When The nuts are fully formed in early autumn, and may stay good well into winter
Tips Outer husks can be used for dye and a tea that acts as a de-worming medicine

ELDERBERRY

Calories 106 calories per cup (100 g)
Nutrients The berries are high in vitamin B6, vitamin C, calcium, iron, and potassium
Where Sunny areas, throughout the northern hemisphere
When Early to mid-summer
Tips Don't munch on the leaves, stem or green berries; most parts are toxic except for the ripe berries

DANDELION

Calories 25 calories per cup (75 g)
Nutrients Loaded with vitamins A, C, and K, along with a small amount of most other necessary minerals
Where Disturbed ground, lawns, fields, and open areas, worldwide
When Year-round
Tips Use yellow flower heads in your salad or roast the roots as a coffee alternative

RASPBERRY

Calories 64 calories per cup (125 g)
Nutrients One cup has 54% of your daily vitamin C and 12% of your daily vitamin K
Where Open areas throughout the northern hemisphere
When Early to the middle of summer
Tips Raspberries are a close relative of the blackberry, and their leaves can also make a tea

CHERRY

Calories 77 calories per cup (150 g)
Nutrients 40% of your Vitamin A; 26% of your daily requirement of Vitamin C; and some potassium, copper, and manganese
Where Forest edges and old fields, throughout the northern hemisphere
When Early, mid, or late summer, depending on the species
Tips Don't swallow cherry pits or eat the leaves, as these are poisonous

PERSIMMON

Calories 127 calories per cup (225 g)
Nutrients One cup provides a full day's vitamin C
Where Old fields and transition areas, throughout the eastern and central U.S.
When Early to mid-fall
Tips Pick only the wrinkled and gooey fruits; unripe ones give you a strong case of cotton mouth

PAW PAW

Calories 80 calories per cup (150 g)
Nutrients One cup has 18% of your daily recommended vitamin C and about 10% of your daily potassium
Where Floodplains and forests throughout the eastern and central U.S.
When Late summer or very early fall
Tips The wood is excellent for friction fire material, and the bark can be used as tinder and cordage

ROSE HIPS

Calories 162 calories per cup (100 g)
Nutrients One cup provides the vitamins A, C, E, and K, as well as some calcium, magnesium, and manganese
Where Sunny areas, throughout the northern hemisphere
When Early fall
Tips Rose hips are a powerhouse when it comes to vitamin C, containing seven times your daily allowance in one cup

BLUEBERRY

Calories 84 calories per cup (100 g)
Nutrients One cup contains one quarter of your daily vitamin C and one third of your vitamin K
Where These bushes and their relatives can grow in a wide range of temperate climates
When Mid to late summer
Tips Regular consumption is believed to improve vision, and eating dried berries can help stop diarrhea

AMARANTH

Calories 716 calories per cup (250 g)
Nutrients There are 26 grams of protein, 30% of your daily calcium, and a full day's iron in one cup
Where Fields and open ground throughout North America
When Late summer or early fall
Tips Seeds can be boiled into a cooked grain or ground into flour; the leaves are edible raw or cooked

GRAPES

Calories 100 calories per cup (100 g)
Nutrients Wild grapes provide good amounts of vitamin C, vitamin K, copper, and potassium
Where Woods and wood edges, throughout the northern hemisphere
When Mid-summer to mid-fall
Tips Grapes have one to four teardrop-shaped seeds, while the toxic moonseed has only one seed which is curved and flat

WILD RICE

Calories 170 calories per cup (250 g)
Nutrients Traces of many vitamins and minerals, and 7 grams of protein
Where Wetlands, throughout the northern U.S. and southern Canada
When Early fall
Tips Harvest from an open canoe, bending the seed heads into the boat and tapping them with a stick

131 WORK WITH BIRCH

If you're lucky enough to have birch trees in your area, then you have a lot of interesting materials at your disposal. Most birch can provide you with firewood and containers—and some species can even yield delicious tea and syrup.

MAKE FIRE The best fire-related use of birch is to burn the papery curls as a fire starter, a kind of stepping-stone between tinder and kindling. Whether they're wet or dry, a match or lighter will ignite birch-bark curls They burn hot, with a black, oily smoke. Any birch species that produces papery bark will be usable, but the white birch (aka paper birch) is the most effective.

CREATE CONTAINERS It's relatively easy to make bowls and dishes from the birch's flexible, rot-resistant bark. Bigger things like canoes are a lot more work to build, but are lightweight and long-lasting. The bark can be peeled from rotten logs or cut from live branches and trunks during the spring bark-peeling season.

BREW TEA Shave off a few strips of bark from a young branch, or break up some twigs into small sticks. About a tablespoon of material will be plenty for a cup of tea with the rich, sweet scent of evergreen (though you'll probably want to drink more than just one cup). This tea can be made any time of year, but if made in early spring when the sap is running, it's naturally sweetened by the sugar in sap. Let the bark shavings or twigs sit in the water for a few hours for the full sweetening effect. Any birch can also be tapped for sap to be boiled down, just like maple syrup.

132 HANDLE HICKORY

Hickory is a species of deciduous hardwood tree found across North America and Asia. If you can break into the armored nuts, the nut meats of most species are rich, oily, and pecan-flavored. But there's a lot more to these trees.

BUILD A BOW Hickory is one of the best woods for bow staves—flexible, rugged, and quick to snap back into shape. Collect slender sapling trees, growing in close competition with other trees, for tight growth rings and straighter staves.

TAP A HICKORY In late winter, drill a small hole into a hickory tree and hammer in a spile, a conical tube that directs the sap flow and allows you to hang a container. Collect your sap as each container fills, and boil down the sap outdoors (too much steam for indoors) until you have a syrup. February is the best month of sap production for most tree species; it takes 30 to 50 quarts (28 to 47 l) of sap to produce one quart of syrup, but it's well worth the trouble.

MAKE BARK SPICE "Spice" is a loosely used term for this one, but it's the closest fit. Shag bark and shell bark hickory (*Carya ovata* and *Carya laciniosa*) are native trees to eastern and central United States. Their loose, exfoliating bark can be stripped off and simmered in milk to add a flavor similar to vanilla. This milk can be used to churn out ice cream, or if it's too cold for that, eggnog. You can even use the flavored milk in your baked goods to bring a taste of the wild indoors.

133 MAKE SOMETHING FROM MULBERRY

These fruits are found around the world, with black, white, and red varieties. Be sure the fruits are ripe and sweet: eating under-ripe mulberries can lead to serious reactions including vomiting, diarrhea, and hallucinations. Here are some uses for the berries, and a bonus one for the bark.

MAKE WINE Mix mulberries, sugar, and water, then boil. After the mix cools and is strained into a sterile glass jug, add red wine yeast and ferment in a dark, room-temperature spot for six weeks. Enjoy the new wine right away, or for best taste, bottle the wine and age for a few months.

SIP ON SYRUP Beautiful purple syrup can be made from mulberries to pour on pancakes, ice cream, or other foods. Mash 1 pint (475 ml) of berries in a pot, add 2 cups (480 ml) of white sugar, and boil for 10 minutes, no water needed. Stir constantly to prevent burning. While the mix is hot, strain it into a clean jar. This is your finished syrup! Store it in the fridge for up to two months.

BAIT YOUR TRAPS Collect a few mulberries when they are abundant, and use them for trap bait where they are scarce. They will draw raccoons, opossums, and even skunks. Just don't bait under a fruiting tree; animals will never go for your bait when there are plenty of berries available.

DYE AND STAIN Black mulberries provide a reddish-purple dye or stain for wood, cloth, or leather. Mash the berries and wipe them on the object for the simplest procedure, though this tends to wash out. Boil the mashed berries in a little water with a mordant, like alum, to brighten the colors and help them stain deeper and better.

TWIST UP CORD Mulberry's inner bark is a very strong fiber, stripped from dead branches once the bark has loosened, or peeled from live branches in spring, and used as a strong rope, cord, or thread. Twist it into two- or three-ply cordage, or use it as-is for quick tying jobs.

134 PICK A PERSIMMON

American and Asian persimmons are closely related; the species found in Japan bears much larger fruits. and neighboring countries. Both have a small woody "cap" with four points, just above the fruit—which isn't the only useful part.

BREW SOME TEA While the fruit is great, there are other things you can do with this small tree. The green leaves can be dried and then steeped for slightly spicy tea. These are best used after a gentle drying process, preferably in the shade. But if time is lacking, the green leaves can be used to brew a nice cup of caffeine-free herbal tea.

MAKE A MALLET The wood of persimmon trees is rock-hard, making excellent mallets and tool handles. The straight-grained white wood is dense, tight, and durable. If you're looking for a new tool handle that will outlast you, go find some persimmon wood.

PREDICT THE WEATHER Folk wisdom has it that persimmon seeds can foretell how harsh a winter will be. Cut the seed in half with a sharp knife and look at the "sprout" inside. If the sprout is skinny like a knife, the winter will be colder than normal. If it's forked, the worst of the weather will split and go around your area, and if it's wide at the end, like a spoon, you'll be scooping lots of snow this winter. There's not a lot of science here, but why not?

ANIMAL FOODS

Taking an animal should be done with restraint, gratitude, and respect. In many different habitats and seasons, animal resources are necessary for long-term survival, and all parts have value. It doesn't make sense to squander anything in a survival situation, and it doesn't respect the life that has been taken. If your life depends on that animal, the feeling of appreciation can be overwhelming.

135 BE A REALIST

Just because you're hungry doesn't mean wild animals are going to show up by the fire to slow roast. In a real survival event, you're more likely to be dining on worms, grubs, small bony fish, small birds, and other less desirable fare.

SET YOUR EXPECTATIONS If you're lucky, a fish, bird, or mammal—or even a nest full of eggs—may fall into your lap. This is the feast-and-famine cycle that our ancestors once lived by. Some days there is excess food, but most days there isn't enough. This is the reality of the hunter-gatherer life, and your expectations should match your skills, supplies, and situation.

KNOW THE ODDS Your survival kit contains a short strand of thin wire, but you won't catch a big animal with it on your first day. And there's a reason they call it "fishing" instead of "catching." Trapping? That's a numbers game. Even with the right bait in the right trap in the right spot, you may not catch anything. Reality can be a bitter pill to swallow, and some days that may be the only thing in your stomach.

136 GO WITH A PRO

If you've never trapped, fished, or hunted before, there's no shame in this knowledge gap. We all had to learn sometime. You can learn a great deal from books, but that only relates someone else's experiences instead of learning yourself. You may be able to muddle through and learn to how to take wild game by yourself, but there's no faster way to learn than to go out there with someone who really knows what they are doing.

If you're lucky, you'll know some grizzled elder willing to take you out. If not, broaden the net and try to find a trustworthy friend of a friend to take you trapping, fishing, or hunting. Failing that, hire a guide to show you the ropes. In all of these cases, pay close attention to their stories, every tip and trick they share, and most importantly, any safety lessons they may have. These safety tips are vital information, particularly when you are unfamiliar with the skills and tools to take down big game. Pay attention to the teachers that you find, and who knows— someday you may be sharing your own wealth of wisdom with a newcomer.

BUSHCRAFT USES FOR ANTLERS

In the long dark winters of the past, our forebears carved useful and beautiful objects from a substance much harder than wood. Antler was an especially important material for Native Americans and for people in the European Late Paleolithic era. Happily, you don't have to stab a monster buck with a spear to get your hands on some antler. Many deer and related species (like moose) shed their antlers each year after the rut is complete. Hunting for these "sheds" can be a fun winter pastime, and your finds will yield a hard and durable substance that can serve many roles.

❶ HANDLES Knives, files, spark rods, and plenty of other tools can be fitted with antler handles to create one-of-a-kind implements that are both beautiful and durable. Individual tines can be used for smaller items, while antler bases can provide a beefy grip for larger tool handles.

❷ CHISELS For working softwood, or even soapstone, an antler chisel is a great tool. Even though it needs frequent sharpening, this tool can be used with a hammer or mallet to successfully carve soft materials.

❸ WHISTLE If you're good at carving (and have right tools), you can turn those antler stubs and scraps into shrill little whistles. These are not usually as loud as their store-bought kin, but any whistle is a good thing to have with you when you're trying to signal your distress or location.

❹ SOCKET For an outstanding friction fire socket, drill a small depression into a rounded chunk of antler, or a flattened antler base. This type of socket is ideal for bow and drill fire starting. It's also a great companion to stone-tipped drills for hole drilling. Use a greasy lubricant with this socket, just as you would with any other porous socket material. And don't be shocked when it gets hot. Antler heats up more quickly than stone or wooden handhold sockets.

5 BUTTONS AND TOGGLES These likely aren't lifesavers, but they are long-lasting and rugged. They also look really cool. Tine tips are ready to go as toggles, and larger sections of antler can be cut into a variety of button shapes and styles.

6 PRESSURE FLAKERS Even little 6-inch (15-cm) antlers can give you enough of a point to use the tines as pressure flakers—the pointy tools used to chip arrowheads and fabricate other stone tools.

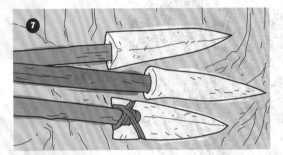

7 PROJECTILE POINTS Sharpened antler tine tips can be glued into place as arrowheads and spear tips. These may be the fixed parts of a projectile, or detachable (like a harpoon toggle). While they can never be sharpened to a razor edge, these tips can still be honed to a vicious point.

8 CONTAINERS From the powder measures for blackpowder shooting, to cases used for protect your precious few needles, antler can be drilled into hollow containers. I use a hollowed antler tine tip for my powder measure when shooting muzzle loaders. It's beautiful and traditional.

9 TRAPS Building small, intricate trap triggers can be very frustrating, especially when you're using wood that keeps breaking. But if you have a few scraps of antler, you can use the same tools to carve much more durable trigger components from antler. Notches, pins, and many other trap mechanisms may outlast you when you carve them from antler.

137 RATTLE ANTLERS

Want to see two antlers turn into four? If you're a hunter, you may be able to lure in a cautious buck by simulating a fight on his turf. Rattling is most productive during the rut, when bucks are more aggressive. While this technique may draw in an amorous doe, it's more likely to draw a defensive buck who assumes that two other bucks are fighting. Some bucks may blindly charge at the sound of the mock battle, while wiser ones creep toward the noise. Either way, try these steps to help you maximize the effectiveness of your rattling.

STEP 1 Before rattling, check the wind direction. Many bucks approach the sound of a fight from downwind, so take every precaution to minimize your scent.

STEP 2 Work up to the big battle. Start your rattling slowly and quietly, clacking and twisting the antlers together. Rattle them lightly for only about 90 seconds to avoid frightening off nearby deer, then wait 5 minutes before making another sound. For round two, go about 2 minutes, hitting the antlers harder to make the sound louder. Wait 30 minutes before rattling again, to give a cautious buck time to move closer.

STEP 3 Before rattling again, rake the ground or scrape the antlers against a tree trunk to simulate a victorious buck marking his new territory. Wait a half hour before moving to a new location, as you may have a wily buck creeping in to get a look.

138 WEIGH YOUR OPTIONS

There are many different types of traps used throughout the world, but they all have something in common. They are some kind of device designed to catch, kill, or retain animals, or at least catch hold of a part of the body. Traps sit out there day and night, even in temperatures and conditions where we wouldn't last too long. And when everything goes right, these contraptions can catch an animal for us.

Of course, these devices aren't foolproof. Traps can malfunction and animals can outsmart them. To maximize your success, you'll want to learn which traps to use, where to put them, how to bait them, and what to do when the trap doesn't work. For this section, we'll focus on the two trap types that are the most practical to build and use in a survival setting—the snare and the deadfall.

139 LOSE THE SMELL

When setting a trap, you don't want to leave a trace of human scent that will scare off prey. Thankfully, there are ways that you can minimize scent, using materials you'll find in nature.

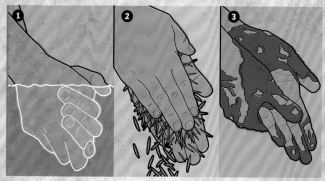

STEP 1 Scrub your hands in a local water source, using sand or mud instead of soap. This removes dead skin flakes and skin oils, and provides the smell of the waterway.

STEP 2 Next, scrub pine needles (or some other pungent nontoxic local plant) all over your hands.

STEP 3 Finally, wipe on a layer of dirt to hide your scent with the two other odors. Be sure to de-scent your hands before you start building trap components, and before handling traps or trap parts, and before setting any traps.

140 KNOW THE LAW

In a true survival situation, you're probably not going to worry too much about the rules and regulations for fishing, hunting, or trapping. In fact, you'd probably welcome an officer of the law to take you to lockup, since it means you've been rescued from the wild.

But if you're practicing all of your bushcraft skills for fun, it is your responsibility to be aware of the legalities in your county, state, and nation. There may be many legal methods of taking wild game in your area, but it doesn't mean that you can do whatever you like. Each area will have its own regulations about the hunting, fishing, and trapping practices, and they may be very different from a neighboring region. These laws are generally in place for good reasons, and unless it's an emergency situation, those laws apply to you.

Learn what you are required to do to take wild game, so you don't run afoul of the game wardens. Get a license. Get written permission from the landowner if you are on private land. And obey the season, as certain animals are only legal to take at certain times.

141 BE A BETTER TRAPPER

There are many reasons to add trapping to your survival skill set. It's a great way to take game animals that are not practical to hunt (such as nocturnal ones); to maximize your chances of getting game; and to take animals when you're not even present. In both wilderness survival and long-term disaster scenarios, trapping makes a lot of sense. Here are four staples of trapping success.

MAKE YOUR PICK Trapping begins with knowing which animal you're after. How will you know which trap or bait to use if you don't pick a target species? How will you know the right place to trap if you don't learn about your quarry? Pick one locally abundant species and learn about its behavior. This will give you a great start for your trap line.

USE QUALITY TRAPS The embarrassment that passes for "trapping gear" in most store-bought survival kits is not useful. Sorry; 10 inches (25 cm) of hair-thin brass wire won't make a snare. Use braided steel cable and metal slide locks.

BE EXCLUSIVE If a variety of species are present at a trapping site, use baits that exclude nontarget species. These will obviously vary, but they will only draw your target critter, not the others.

LET THE SNOW WORK FOR YOU If you're careless, your traps can be hopelessly buried beneath the snows. Try some sets on large, angled logs that rise up out of the snow, exposed rock outcrops, and other high points for animals to run above the snow. Snow can be a trapper's friend, if you let it. Snow covers up animal food sources and can even hinder their travel. This can make your bait even more appealing and make the path to toward it seem like a natural choice.

142 AVOID YOUR OWN TRAPS

There are lots of ways to hurt yourself badly when working with traps. In a survival situation, you can't afford to make any mistakes that could take you out of the game. If your trap can hurt (or kill) an animal, then that trap can hurt the trapper too (that's you!). Here are three things to avoid when setting survival traps.

AVOID DEADFALL DESTRUCTIONS I can't even count the number of times that a deadfall weight has landed on my knuckles while I was tweaking a trigger. You can prevent this by putting a fist-sized stone or chunk of wood under the deadfall, but don't interfere with the trigger. Leave this in place while setting the trap. If the trigger goes off unexpectedly, the rock or log will hit your "safety" instead of your hand. Once the trap and trigger are set, remove the obstruction.

DON'T HOLD THE NOOSE Spring-pole snares must be strong and quick to catch and dispatch game, but it's dangerous to handle them. Never get your fingers near a set noose. If it springs unexpectedly it can skin your fingers or hand. If you need to maneuver the noose after the trigger is set, use long sticks to move it.

SKIP THE SPRING-POLE SLAP I've had the end of a sapling pole break and slap me in the head. When setting a spring-pole snare, stay under the arch, not outside it. If the trigger goes off unexpectedly while you're kneeling under the arch, the pole rises up and away from you.

The simplicity of the Paiute deadfall makes it one of my favorite traps. You can make it with just a few sticks and a bit of string, providing there are plenty of flat rocks available. To put it together, you'll need a Y-shaped stick for the vertical post, a straight stick for the lever, a short stick to be the toggle, a slender bait stick, a piece of string, some bait, and a big flat rock.

Assemble it by tying one end of the string to the lever, and the other end to the toggle. Wipe or skewer the bait on the bait stick, and stand up the "Y" stick by the edge of the rock. Put the stringless end of the lever in the fork of the "Y" stick and place the rock on the tip. Wrap the toggle halfway around the post, and pin the bait stick between the rock and the toggle.

This is the basic trap construction, but you don't have to stop there. Here are two ways to ramp up the power of your deadfall trap.

EXTRA WEIGHT Can't find a flat rock that's heavy enough for your target species? Use the widest rock you can find, set up your trap, and gently start adding more stones on top of your flat rock to ramp up the overall weight of the trap.

SPRING POLES These add more force and speed to your deadfall. Lay one or two springy branches (two offers more stability) on the ground behind the deadfall, with the ends of the branches across the top of your trap weight. Add a few large rocks or logs on top of the branches to pin them down and put their springiness into action.

144 BAIT A STICK SNARE

This snare is great for most small game animals and most occasions. You'll need a strong, flexible sapling for the spring pole, a forked stake, a slender toggle stick, a snare line, a toggle line, a bait stick, and some bait.

STEP 1 Trim the branches and leaves from your spring pole, then tie the snare line

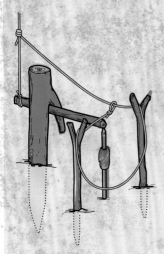

to the end of it. Bend the pole until the snare line touches the ground and mark that spot. A braided steel snare cable is the best, but rope will work if the trap is fast enough to kill.

STEP 2 Drive the forked stake into the ground on the marked spot. This keeps the snare line plumb, which is vital to setting the trap. Tie your pencil toggle to the end of the trigger line.

STEP 3 Run the toggle under the fork on the stake in the ground, keeping the toggle parallel to the ground and at a right angle to the stake. Set your baited trigger stick out at the end of the toggle, which should set the entire trap. Use a stick to set it off and test it. If it springs up quickly, set some twigs to support the noose, and reset the trigger, but keep your hands away from the noose.

145 TRAP WITH A TREE

In sandy soils and other substrates that won't hold a stake in the ground, use an anchoring system with deeper roots, namely a small tree or bush. Set up your main spring pole near a smaller woody plant. Bend the little guy over and weigh it down with a rock or log, so that it makes a small arch. Treat this arch just like the stake in the ground on the bait stick snare. The deep roots will hold better than you might imagine.

CAVEMAN'S CORNER

146 GRAB SOME WILD BAIT

When it comes to trapping, you often need specific baits to lure in certain animals. That's why the art of baiting traps is so important. The wrong bait can leave you with an empty trap over and over; the right bait can mean that you get fed.

So how do you get bait when you're stuck in the wilderness? Pick an animal to trap, figure out what its diet consists of, and try to find that bait. Use some wild fruits that are out of reach for the rabbits. Rip open a rotten log and pull out some grubs to feed omnivores. And use the organ meat from a trapped animal to catch fresh-meat loving carnivore. Determine what your target species would like to eat, and give it to them.

147 GO BAIT-FREE

If you're lacking in the bait department, then take bait out of the equation. Tie your noose line to the bait stick, and then set the noose in a rabbit run or some other small pathway (not a major game trail). When the animal gets caught in the noose and pulls on it, they are also pulling the trap trigger.

148 BUILD A SURVIVAL FISHING KIT

If you want to be prepared should you need to catch some fish for emergency sustenance, a pocket-sized fishing kit does the trick. Basic gear includes a small coil of monofilament line, some small weights, and an assortment of hooks. With these simple supplies, you can catch plenty of fish, and it's easy to carry anywhere.

HOOKS There may not be a big fish in every wilderness waterway, but there are almost always some little ones. And a little fish cannot bite a big hook. For best results, pack some small and medium-sized hooks, along with a few larger ones, in your kit. This way you can handle a wide range of fish sizes and species.

LINE Monofilament fishing line is a modern marvel. It's strong, lightweight, stretchy and apparently it's hard for the fish to see. Some 50 yards (or meters) of 10lb (.260 mm) test would work well for most kits. Fishing line is usually bundled tightly to save space in survival fishing kits. Don't do this! The line will take on the bends and twists of its bundling, making it a nightmare to unwind and cast. Instead, store your line in the largest round coils your survival kit will allow.

WEIGHTS A dozen little split shot weights can make a big difference in your survival fishing game. Select weights that can be crimped and removed easily by hand. They take up so little space, but make such a big difference in your casting ability. They are well worth the small additional weight to your kit.

149 CUT A FISHING POLE

If you have hooks, line, and weights, then adding a fishing pole to your tackle is the next logical choice. Here's how you can make a pole in three easy steps.

STEP 1 Find a flexible hardwood sapling, about thumb thickness at the base and 2 to 3 yards (meters) long. Look for a slender young tree growing in a thick tangle of brush. The tree will be skinny but strong from competing with other vegetation, and you'll be doing the other plants a service by removing it.

STEP 2 Cut the tree with any tool you have. An axe, a saw, or even a pocket knife will work.

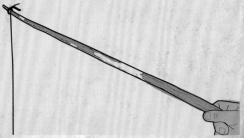

STEP 3 Trim off all branches and tie your fishing line to the slender end of pole. Now you're ready to go fishing!

150 FIND YOUR OWN BAIT

Fishing with hook and line won't be very effective unless you find tasty critters to use as bait. For successful fish traps and fishing with hook and line, your best bet is to select irresistible bait. Since most fish species are carnivores, it's hard to go wrong with worms, grubs, crickets and other natural bug bait.

FLIP OVER A ROCK
One of the easiest ways to find bait is to flip over stones and other solid objects. These protected habitats often have worms, slugs, grubs, and many other fine bait bugs hiding underneath them.

RIP OPEN A LOG Grubs and beetles often make their home in rotten logs. Tear into the soft punky wood with tools or with your bare hands. Pick through the crumbled pieces to collect your prizes. Not only are these creatures a tempting treat for fish, but they make a valuable survival food for hungry humans too. Just cook your bugs until well done for safety.

DISTURB THE DIRT Worms are often upset by vibrations in the ground, and these disturbances can make them head for the surface. Pound a rock or pole against the ground, and watch for any worms that may start squirming their way skyward. Similarly, an old-timey trick is to scut notches into a walking sticks, and then rub another stick up and down on the notches to send the vibrations into the soil. These old fashioned tricks don't always work, but they're worth a try. I have seen them work firsthand (some of the time!).

151 IMPROVISE A FISH WEIR

Fish traps have been used by people around the world for a very long time; the biggest such trap is the fish weir. Since these traps are working hard to collect food for you day and night, they can really make an impact on your food gathering efforts.

So if you want to get serious about fishing, and going to be in one spot for a while, add a fish weir to your food collection plan. A weir can be a "V" shaped wall or a circular fence that either direct fish into smaller fish traps or simply confine them within the weir. Some of the traditional weir construction styles of ancient times are still being used today.

Weirs can be built of stone for permanent construction. They can also be made by driving stakes into the mud to create semi-permanent installations. Your weir can take advantage of the flow of a river. And in coastal areas, they can work with the tides—trapping fish as the tide goes out. Weirs can get you as close as you're going to get to "shooting fish in a barrel" in a primitive survival setting.

152 USE YOUR BARE HANDS

The concept of "hand fishing" is simple enough, but it's like many other "simple" survival skills in that it actually requires a lot of technique. Whether "graveling" for catfish or "bug diving" to collect lobsters, you're taking a page from the playbook of our most remote ancestors when you catch aquatic animals with your bare hands.

CATCH A CAT Catfish like to hang out in underwater rock ledges, as well as in holes and under submerged logs. If you reach into these protected spots, the fish will be trapped with its back up against the wall. If all goes right, the fish will advance and bite your hand. Fight your natural urge to pull your hand away; leave your hand in the fish's mouth and pull it toward you. Wrap your free arm around the fish, being careful to avoid contact with the barbs on the fish's fins.

BAG A BUG Likewise, speedy grabs and swatting motions are the most successful methods of snatching a lobster from protected spots in shallow saltwater. Of course, these underwater shelters can also contain sea urchins, moray eels, scorpion fish, and other sea creatures that bite, stab, and sting. Being truly bare handed is a poor choice. Instead, don a pair of Kevlar gloves. These cut-proof, puncture-proof gauntlets protect against urchin spines and many other dangers of the deep. And never go hand fishing alone. You'll want some help if you get injured or your arm is trapped underwater.

153 GO ALL NATURAL

You can catch a fish using cord you've made yourself, and a thorn for a hook. When one of my students catches their first fish using this method, words can't express the feeling of accomplishment in both the teacher and the student. If you'd like to add this experience to your list of bushcraft accomplishments, then follow along.

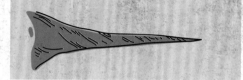

FIND YOUR HOOK Start by finding a sharp, straight thorn on a tree or bush. This can be used as a gorge hook, which will catch a fish by their innards, rather than by their mouth as is the case with steel hooks.

TWIST UP LINE Next, collect the strongest plant fibers you can find. Twist together a thin but strong thread, using the reverse wrap method (see item 233). Twist the cord and splice in new fibers until you have several meters of fishing leader. You can tie this to stouter cord for hand line fishing, or tie it to a long pole for pole fishing.

CATCH A FISH Tie the dull end of your thorn to the end of the line, insert it into a chunk of bait, and cast your line. Let the fish take the bait, but do not jerk the line to set the hook. Once you think the fish has swallowed the bait, coax it into a waiting net, very slowly.

154 KNIT A NET

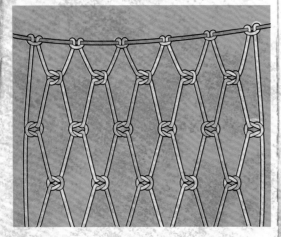

The oldest known fishing net dates back to about 8,300 BCE. Made of willow bark, it was found with other fishing tackle at an archaeological dig in Finland. Net weaving is a complicated and precise art, but it can also be dead simple. With an ample supply of cordage, you can try your hand at this age-old craft.

STEP 1 Tie a thin rope between two points, like a pair of trees. The length of the rope will determine the maximum width of the net, and the height of the rope will determine the maximum height of the net (but you can always stop short).

STEP 2 Along this rope, tie long pieces of cord using a lark's head hitch (the beginning of a Prusik knot in item 035). Space them closely together. At each hitch, you want to have equal lengths of cord hanging down.

STEP 3 Begin to tie knots in the hanging cords. You can use square knots, or other knots, as you prefer. Use your fingers or some object as a spacing gauge, to make sure that every opening in the net is roughly the same size. Don't weave back and forth. If you're going left to right, for example, tie knots all along, then go back to the left side again and do the next row, going down one more step with each course completed.

STEP 4 When you've reached your target size, or run out of cord, tie off any loose ends and put your net to work.

155 HIT THE SPOT

Looking for food in the water doesn't just mean fishing; clams are yet another food source—one you can get with bare hands!

MIND THE TIDE Go clamming at low tide, when there's more area to dig. Minus tides are best; get to the clam bed 2 hours before peak low tide. During times of less swell, your quarry is likely to be closer to the surface (and your plate) than other times.

LOOK FOR SIGNS A clam's neck near the surface of the sand produces a "show"—a hole, dimple, or indentation. If you don't see this in an area that you're pretty sure has clams, pound your hands or shovel on the sand in receding surf. If you're lucky, this may reveal a show (or even multiple shows).

DIG FAST Some clams are sluggish; others are lightning fast. The Pacific razor clam is one of the swiftest, and it can bury itself faster than some clammers can dig.

156 DOPE UP THE WATER

It's illegal in most places today, but native folks around the world have used plant poisons in fishing. Compounds in numerous plants can stun a fish's respiratory or nervous system, especially in still water. The stupefied fish simply float to the surface to await your collection. Crushed mullein seed, and the bark and green nut husks of black walnut are two examples of plants used for centuries in North America as effective fish poisons. In a small body of water, you can bring up fish that refuse to be caught otherwise. Again, it's illegal and unsportsmanlike, but in a dire emergency, you do what you must. Just catch and gut the fish quickly to minimize exposure to the toxins, and cook it until well done.

157 CARVE A BOW

Making a working bow takes a bit of time, practice, and skill, but it can be done.

❶ PICK THE RIGHT WOOD Archery and bowyering are skills that date back several millennia. Today, they can both be a fun hobby and hunting tools in the wild. But before you grab just any sapling to carve a bow, you need the right wood. Some of the better bow wood species include Osage orange, yew, ash, sycamore, black locust, and hickory, though most any hardwoods (such as oak and maple) can work.

For a quick survival bow, use a relatively straight section of sapling or branch free of knots, side branches, and twists, about 6 feet (2 m) long and about 2 inches (5 cm) in diameter. This piece is now your bow stave. For same-day shooting, it should be dead and dry, with no rot. Live-cut wood is a poor choice, but you can cut staves and dry them indoors for a few months.

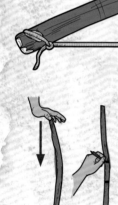

❷ FIND THE BELLY AND BACK First, stand the bow stave straight up, hold the top loosely with one hand, and push on the middle to bend it. The stave should swivel to show you which way it wants to bend. The outside is the "back"; the inside bend is the "belly." Leave the back untouched. Mark out a handhold area in the middle of the bow by measuring and marking about 3 inches (8 cm) out from the center in both directions. The handhold area will also be left untouched. The area above the handhold is the upper limb and the area below is the lower limb. Use a marker or charcoal to mark out the handhold, belly, and back for reference while carving. For balance, most people make and shoot these bows mirroring the way the tree or branch grew—with the thicker base as the lower limb.

❸ CARVE WITH CARE Bend your bow and carefully study how each limb moves. Begin removing wood from the stiffer parts of the belly using a knife, drawknife, or stone scraper. Rake care to leave material in the areas of the limbs that already bend a lot. It's very common to remove more wood from the thicker end of the stave, and less wood from the thinner. Only remove wood from the belly side of the limbs; you should be leaving the back untouched. The goal at this step is to get the limbs to start bending equally. Take off material slowly and recheck the bend of the limbs frequently. You will be ready for the next step when both limbs flex evenly throughout their length.

4 STRING IT UP Carefully saw some small notches on both sides of each tip—they only need to be deep enough to keep a bow string in place. Tie loops into both ends of a nylon, sinew, paracord, or plant fiber string. You'll want about 5 to 6 inches (13 to 15 cm) of space between the string and the handhold when the bow is strung. Don't fully draw the bow yet, as this may break it.

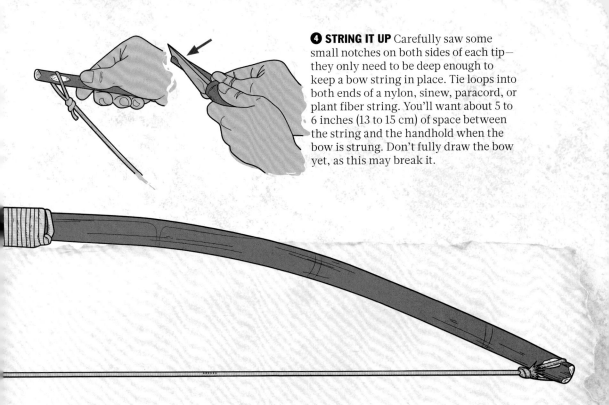

5 DO THE FINISH WORK For final shaping and tillering, hang the bow up horizontally on a tree branch by the handhold. Now pull down a few inches on the string while observing how the limbs bend. You want each limb to bend evenly throughout its length, and by exactly the same amount, mirroring each other. Shave, scrape, sand, or carve the belly of each limb until they do bend equally and evenly, all the way to the full draw length of the bow.

158 DON'T BREAK IT!

There are so many ways you can destroy your field-built bow. Trust me: If you decide to make stuff, you're going to break stuff. With a little bit of practice, however, you'll learn to avoid a lot of these mistakes, and keep others from breaking your hard-earned bow.

PROTECT YOUR BELLY The number-one mistake that I see new bowyers make is chopping into one spot too deeply on the belly of the bow. It's only natural—they're excited and inexperienced. They want to make the bow quickly, so they are chopping away like a lumberjack felling a tree. But you shouldn't be chopping at all. Just take off careful slices and shavings, and make sure that no area gets too thin while you continue carving. Otherwise, the back will break when the bow is drawn.

SAVE THE BACK Don't hurt the back of your bow. Don't carve designs into it. Don't try to trim off material. This is the side under tension when the bow is drawn, and it doesn't take much to create a bow-breaking weak spot.

159 FLETCH SOME ARROWS

The bow may be a little tricky for beginners to make, but ultimately, the arrows are the complicated part. They must be as perfect as possible, since inconsistencies can send them sailing off course and away from your target. Each finished arrow needs to be lightweight, strong, straight, and well-fletched, and have the right rigidity (spine) and length for the bow you are shooting. Follow these steps for aerodynamic arrows.

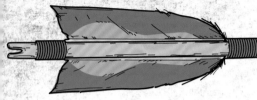

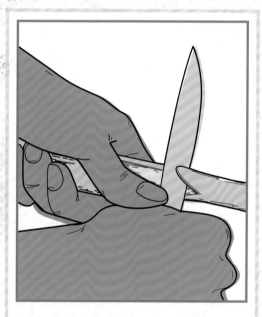

STEP 1 Collect branches, woody shoots, and straight saplings that are at least 30 inches (75 cm) long with diameters between ⅜ inch and ½ inch (around 1 cm). If making arrows in the field, carefully peel the bark off and set the wood aside for a few days to dry. If you are making arrows later, bundle the shafts tightly together with string and set them in a dry place for a few months.

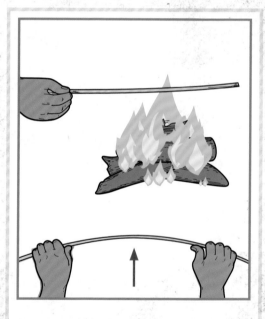

STEP 2 Remove any bark remnants and sand the shafts smooth. Then straighten them by bending them over an open fire. To do this, heat a crooked area (don't let it change color or burn), and bend it a little past straight. Hold the wood in that position until it cools. It should spring back to the desired shape when released. It may take several cycles of heating and cooling to get the shaft straight.

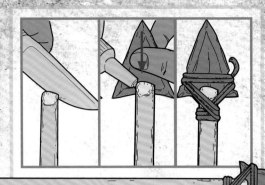

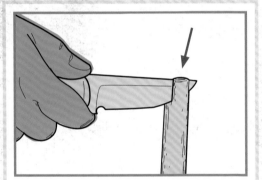

STEP 4 Make simple arrowheads from thin iron or steel, carved bone shards, or chipped pieces of stone. These should be triangular shaped and about 1 ½ to 2 inches (4 to 5 cm) in length and about 1 inch (2.5 cm) wide. Glue the arrowhead into a notch, similar to a bowstring nock, and wrap fine cordage or fibers. Seal the wrapping with pine pitch or more glue to make sure the arrowhead and the wrappings stay in place.

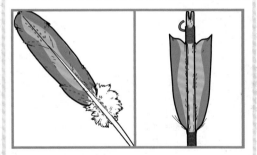

STEP 3 Cut the nock (the notch for the bowstring) about ¼ inch (.75 cm) deep into the end of the shaft. Make sure that the nock is carefully cut out so as to avoid splitting the arrow. Reinforce it by tying string around the shaft, below the nock cut.

STEP 5 Gather bird feathers and split them in half. The feathers need to be from either the wing or the tail for each arrow, not mix and match. They must also be from the same side of the bird (right or left). Trim them to about 4 to 5 inches (11 to 13 cm) long and about ½ inch (1 cm) wide. Space three feathers around the arrow equally, glue them in place, and secure with the same cord as the arrowhead. Cover the fletching fronts so the sharp ends of the quills don't poke out. Warning: Never use a wooden arrow with a compound bow; they can literally explode when fired.

160 FIRE HARDEN A SPEAR

Fire hardening is a frequently misunderstood concept. Most people think that fire hardens wood by some kind of structural change. But in truth, fire hardening is simply the act of "super drying" the wood. Just like bread, dry is hard; moist is soft. There's no secret recipe either. To fire harden wood, bone, or antler, simply turn the item over the fire, just above the flames, until it starts to get a little color. Here's how you can use what nature provides to build a spear.

FIND THE WOOD Start with a sapling tree growing in dense, shady conditions. This will give you a staff with dense wood and tight growth rings. The ready-to-go size will also save you lots of carving work. Choose live wood or a recently deceased sapling for your spear.

GIVE IT SOME HEAT Carve a point on the smaller end (or both ends) and make it as sharp as you can. Rotate the carved area above a small fire to dry the wood. Once it has a "toasted" look, you're done. Imagine you're trying to toast a marshmallow. It should be golden brown, with little to no black char. You can resharpen the point after hardening.

161 HAVE A JAVELIN

While thrusting spears are meant to be handheld, the javelin is a throwing spear. Thrusting spears are usually made with the heavier end as the grip and the slender end as the point. You'll want to reverse this, placing the weight forward on a javelin. Carve your point on the end that was closest to the sapling's roots, in order to give you a front-weighted projectile, which is easier to throw. To stabilize its flight even further, you can also add three or four fletchings to the skinny end of the javelin.

162 MAKE AN ATLATL

Used since the Middle Paleolithic times, the atlatl is a spear-throwing set that can launch a small spear (called a dart) more than 100 yards (meters). Traditional cultures have used these weapons on large and small game, as well as fish. Dart speeds of up to 93 mph (150 km/h) have been recorded with modern examples of this weapon. With practice, it's surprisingly accurate to distances of 20 yards (meters). It's also surprisingly easy to make.

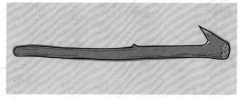

STEP 1 Select a small hardwood branch about a 18 inches (0.5 m) long, with a small side branch. Cut off most of the side branch, but leave part of it sticking up as a pointed hook.

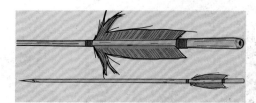

STEP 2 Drill a small cup-shaped depression in the end of a fletched javelin, which should range from 4 to 9 feet (1.2 to 2.7 m) in length and about a ½ inch (1.25 cm) in diameter.

STEP 3 Set the cup of the dart onto the thrower hook, pinch the dart in thumb and index finger, and hold the thrower tight with the rest. Move the thrower forward quickly and release the "pinch grip."

163 TRY SPEAR FISHING

This traditional arctic fish spear (sometimes called a leister) is highly effective. The forked spear's angled opening funnels fish into the center prong. When this spear is thrust, the fish is impaled with all three points. This unique spear gives its user a greater margin of error during their strike, and it helps to account for the fish's movement along with the refraction of the water (which makes the fish look higher than its actual position in the water). This ingenious design gives you the best chance of putting fish in your belly with a spear-fishing technique.

STEP 1 Select a sturdy pole for your spear shaft. It should be thicker than your thumb and as long as you are tall. Also collect wood, bone, antler, or metal pieces for the spear's fork and barbs.

STEP 2 Carve and sharpen the center prong for the spear. Drill a hole in the end of your spear shaft to receive the prong and glue it in place.

STEP 3 Drill and insert the barbs for both sides of the spear fork. Glue and tie the fork pieces in place at the spear's end.

STEP 4 Use the spear by stalking carefully to the water's edge, holding the spear's tip near the surface. When a promising seafood target is spotted, aim below the fish to allow for the refraction of the water and thrust. With any luck, your quarry has been pierced by the three sharp spear points and you'll have fish for dinner.

164 MAKE A SLING

One of smallest and most portable hunting tools that we still have from ancient times is the sling. A bit of string, a patch of cloth or leather, and some round stones are all the equipment required for slaying rabbits and the odd giant or two. The sling is fast and easy to make, and the ammo is literally everywhere. But if you didn't grow up with this weapon as a plaything, you likely haven't thrown the thousands of stones it takes for effective targeting. But you might just be a natural, and practice helps.

STEP 1 Cut two lengths of cord 2 ½ feet (0.75 m) long each. 550 cord is fine, but almost any cord works. Tie a bowline knot in the end of one line, with a big enough loop to slip over your thumb.

STEP 2 Tie three or four knots at the end of the other line. Figure eights or overhands will be fine.

STEP 3 Cut an oval-shaped piece of cloth or leather a little wider than your hand. This will be your sling pad.

STEP 4 Pierce a hole at each point of your sling pad and tie the unknotted ends of your two lines in place. If the sling pad is leather, you can dampen it with water, place a round stone in the pad, and squeeze the stone through the pad for a few minutes to shape the pad for better sling results. The sling is complete. Now comes the hard part: aiming it.

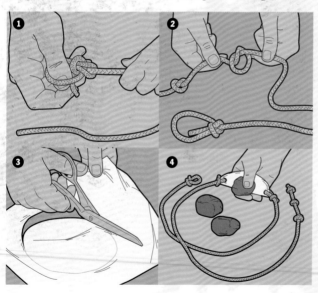

165 AIM THAT THING

Building a sling isn't too difficult, but learning to properly launch stones can be a challenge.

TAKE HOLD Place the bowline loop over the thumb on your throwing hand. Hold the knotted line end between your thumb and palm. Load a rock into the pad. Be sure you hold the knotted line in your palm so that the sling pad is cradling the stone level and even, like a hammock.

SPIN IT UP Try some easy underhand throws first, releasing the knotted line from your hand at the right time to let the rock go sailing. Once you have a feel for when to release the knotted line (which is essentially your trigger on this weapon), you can try a few overhand throws or even overhead circles. Then, try adding more energy to your throw.

PRACTICE A LOT Using a sling can take years to master, as you are trying to instinctively calculate the zenith and azimuth of your target, how much strength to put into that last swing, and the fall on the stone, plus wind. I know, it's too much to actively think about, but with enough practice, you can do it.

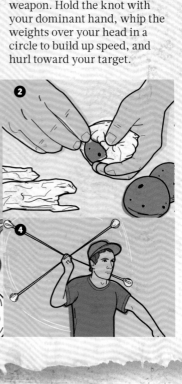

166 ADD SOME SNAP

When you say the words "sling shot," people don't often picture the sling we just discussed. Instead, they imagine a Y-shaped stick with an elastic band to hurl small rocks. This design can be used as a survival sling for small game, and it's not hard to make. A forked stick of hardwood, a small leather patch, a bit of cord, and some surgical tubing are the raw materials for this tool.

STEP 1 Pierce holes on each side of your leather strip and tie a piece of the surgical tubing in place, supplementing the lashing with cord (if needed).

STEP 2 Tie knots in the ends of the tubing, and then tie off the tubing to the forked stick, again using cord to secure it further. Take a few test pulls before you add rocks, just to check all of your knots.

STEP 3 Start testing out the slingshot's power and accuracy. Since this is more like aiming a gun, you may find it a lot easier to aim than the other kind of sling, though typically not as powerful. Still, you may want to start carrying the rubber tubing and leather pad in your survival kit. It could be handy, and you'll likely have fun making and using this hunting tool. You can even shoot arrows with it!

167 BUILD A BOLA

Primarily an impact weapon, the bola can also entangle. A lucky strike stuns or kills the quarry, while the cord ensnares it so you can move in and finish the job. A bola with three to five weights is commonly used in bird hunting; birds' hollow bones are vulnerable to strikes and their wings can be entangled.

Here is how to make your own bola. For stone weights, take care if you skip the rawhide wrap. Even the best lashings and knots can fail over time. Wrap up your stones if at all possible.

STEP 1 Use an overhand knot or a figure-eight knot to join three to five cords; each should be 24 to 32 inches (60 to 80 cm) long.

STEP 2 Collect stones for your weights. They should be about 0.5 pounds (0.25 kg) each. Round stones are less likely to cut through the rawhide.

STEP 3 Wrap the stones in wet rawhide. Pierce a few holes in the edges of the rawhide and fasten each cord to the weight. Let the rawhide fully dry, to shrink and harden, holding the weights securely.

STEP 4 Now it's time to use the weapon. Hold the knot with your dominant hand, whip the weights over your head in a circle to build up speed, and hurl toward your target.

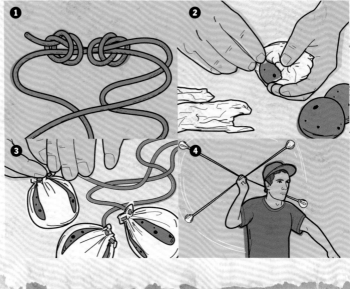

168 GO OUT FOR DINNER

Are you ready for the hunt? Let's see. You've made your weapon. You've spent hours practicing on targets with it. Now it's time to see if your skills are up to the challenge. Hunting is a serious endeavor, and for any chance of success, you'll need to take each one of these skills seriously.

PICK YOUR QUARRY The weapons you've got available may be the determining factor as to what's on the menu (since it's unlikely that you'll kill a deer with a rock). Your environment is another key factor, determining which animals that are available. But you may still get some say in the matter, and you should choose the best quarry that you think you can take in the area.

CHOOSE YOUR WEAPON If you've got multiple options for weapon of choice, pick wisely. Only go out hunting with a weapon that you have spent hours practicing with, and be realistic about whether it's capable of dispatching your intended game animal.

FIND THEIR HABITAT Go where the animals are. Find areas with food, water, and cover for the critters you're seeking. Look for tracks and other sign that the animals present, and find a nearby place to hide that can act as a natural blind.

STAY SILENT Humans are naturally noisy creatures, but that won't do when you're hunting. Walk slowly, don't break twigs, and hold in that sneeze. Be as quiet as a ghost during your hunt.

BE SCENT AWARE As discussed in the trapping section, your scent can be a major alarm to the animal kingdom. Try to minimize it with cover scents, and stay aware of the wind direction. Hunt with the wind in your face, not at your back.

TAKE THE SHOT When everything comes together, you might only have a second or two to take the shot. Move smoothly and don't hesitate. With stunning weapons, you'll need to rush over to finish the job with a bludgeon. But after a fatal projectile shot (arrow, dart or javelin) has hit the animal, watch which way they go and give them a few minutes to pass peacefully. With any luck, the blood trail will lead you to your next meal.

169 AVOID COMMON MISTAKES

Hunting is hard enough when you're doing everything right. And it's near impossible when you make any mistakes. Make sure you don't fall prey to these five common hunting blunders.

NOT SCOUTING YOUR SITE You need to know what's out there before you head out on a hunt.

BEING IMPATIENT Patience is a virtue, and it's an absolute necessity in hunting. Be patient, and you may be rewarded with meat.

IGNORING THE WEATHER A patch of bad weather can cause all of the animals to seek cover, and put you in a hazardous situation. Keep an eye out for a change in the weather if you can't check the forecast before heading out.

BEING UNDERPREPARED You don't want to get caught without enough bullets, enough arrows, enough safety equipment, or enough survival supplies.

FORGETTING ABOUT SCENT Don't forget that many game animals rely on their noses as much as we rely on our eyes. Don't poop or pee in your hunting area. Chew pine needles to hide your breath. De-scent your clothing before the hunt.

170 PROCESS SMALL GAME

Small game animals such as rabbits, squirrels, and possums have been the stew-pot fillers for many people over thousands of years, right up to today. There are plenty of ways to get them all ready for that pot—here's a very easy process that I use frequently.

STEP 1 Cut off the head, feet, and tail.

STEP 2 Cut a slit in the hide (without cutting into the meat), all the way around the animal's mid-section.

STEP 3 Insert two fingers under the hide on each side of the cut at the animal's back and pull hard to peel the hide off.

STEP 4 Cut the belly open from breastbone to backdoor, and scoop out the guts. Save and cook edible innards like the heart, lungs, liver, and kidneys.

STEP 5 Wash off the meat, and cook the animal whole, or cut it into quarters first.

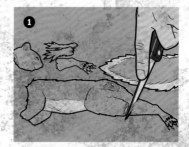
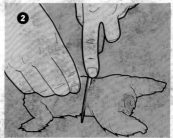
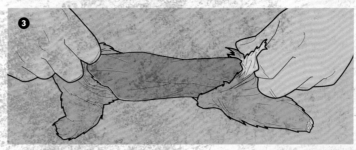

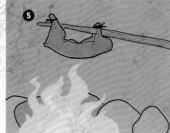

171 CLEAN A FISH

Cleaning a fish may be the easiest game processing job of them all.

A Using a dull knife or a stone scraper, scrape off the scales in short strokes, going from tail to head.

B Scratch your fingernails across the fish skin to find any scales that can't be seen. Finish up your scraping and make a cut from vent to chin.

172 SKIN A SNAKE

Snakes look frightening to some people and mouth-watering to others (yes, the latter is a smaller number of people). Just imagine that snake meat is a very small (yet very long) rack of ribs. Prepare a bed of coals and break out the BBQ sauce—it's time for a snake cookout!

STEP 1 Hold the dead snake down with a forked stick, if necessary, and cut off its head. See the safety box for how to handle venous species.

STEP 2 Slit the belly open and remove the contents. Use these for trap bait or fish bait.

STEP 3 Pull the skin off, and wash the meat.

STEP 3 Cook the snake meat whole or cut into sections. if roasting, don't overcook it, or it will dry out quickly and become very tough to chew. It tastes better roasted, but the meat will be more tender if slow-cooked as a soup or stew.

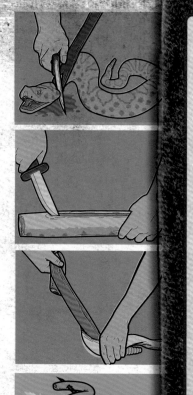

173 BE SAFE!

If you're truly desperate (or if you are a recklessly adventurous gourmet) you can actually eat a number of venomous species. That said, don't even bother with any kind of coral snake. They are simply too dangerous to justify the amount of meat on their bones, and their venom glands run over a quarter of the length of their body.

When preparing a venomous snake to eat, take care to cut its head off at least a few inches back (15 cm) behind the head itself on venomous species, in order to avoid cutting into its venom glands. Bury the head afterward to prevent accidents—a severed snake head can still inject venom if it is stepped on.

C On larger fish, you can make a slice under the chin to detach the gills as well. Pull the gills and innards free.

D Scrape out the dark "vein" on the spine, and remove the head and fins, if desired. (I leave the head in place, as a simple cooking timer.)

174 BUTCHER A BIRD

Birds come apart in a similar way to other game animals. The only major difference is the process of plucking the feathers. A quick dip in scalding hot water will make the plucking process much easier, though you can still do it without this heat treatment. The process described here will work for just about any bird you're likely to bring down.

PLUCK Starting anywhere you like, pinch a few feathers really hard, and pull them out. Move to a neighboring spot and repeat. Do this until the exterior of the bird is feather-free.

START BUTCHERING Remove the bird's head, feet and wing tips. You can opt to do this before plucking, but if they're feather-free these stray parts can be used to make soup stock, so I recommend that option.

GUT YOUR BIRD Once plucked, cut the bird open between "vent" and breastbone, and remove the innards. Save and cook any that you like.

COOK IT UP Roast or boil the bird whole, or cut it up as you would a chicken.

175 CARVE UP BIG GAME

Field dressing involves removal of internal organs, so that the body can cool more quickly and the meat is not tainted.

HOIST Hang the animal from a nearby tree by the neck, so that the guts will just fall right out.

START THE PROCESS Cut around the anus, pull the rectum outward, and tie it off with string. Next, cut through the belly, from ribs to anus.

CUT CAREFULLY When you first pierce into the abdomen, foul gas will escape. Cut around male organs, and remove the abdominal organs. You may have to do some cutting of connective tissue to free the stomach and large intestine.

FINISH UP Cut the diaphragm where it attaches to the rib cage, and remove the heart and lungs.

REPOSITION Hang the carcass head-down for easier butchering. Cut a slit in each rear leg, between the tendon and bone. Tie a rope to each tendon, thread a stout pole through the leg cuts, or use a gambrel hook.

USE AS NEEDED Hang the animal briefly in warm weather, for days in the cold, or weeks in freezing conditions. Leave the hide on to keep out air and insects. Unless you process the whole animal at once, peel it back to remove meat in cold weather, as if it were plastic wrap.

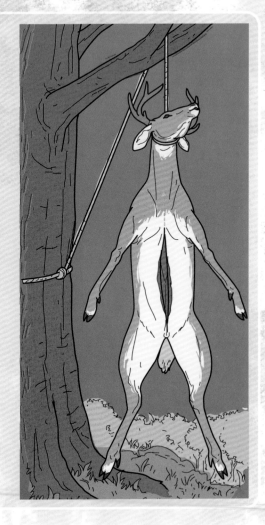

176 KNOW YOUR CUTS

When butchering a deer, even in survival situations, it makes sense to know which cuts are which. This knowledge makes sectioning the beast easier and more systematic, and if you know much about cooking, it should help you determine how to prepare various cuts.

PRO TIP The backstraps are the most choice cut.

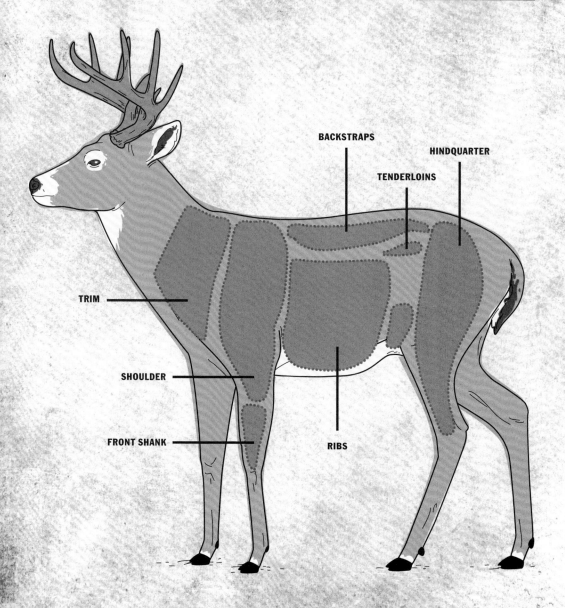

BACKSTRAPS

HINDQUARTER

TENDERLOINS

TRIM

SHOULDER

FRONT SHANK

RIBS

LONG TERM
LIVING

This final chapter is devoted to the traditional living skills of our ancestors, and a few contemporary skills you'd do well to learn for any long-term stay in the wild. Since there's more to survival than just eating raw plants and drinking purified spring water in your primitive hut, this section is packed with handy techniques for making the things you need and tips for how to do without the things you don't. From cooking to making tools to tracking to wild medicine, this chapter will round out your bushcraft skill set and help you to feel more like a native in nature—not just a tourist. The wilderness is an amazing storehouse of resources, if you know how to unlock them.

COOKING

There's more to cooking than just dangling a hunk of meat over a fire. At its heart, cooking is all about transformation. The act of cooking turns nutrient-laden plant and animal parts into something delicious. And in the process of cooking in the wild, we also combine transform sticks, stones, and embers into the tools and means preparing and serving that food.

177 STAY SAFE BY THE FIRE

You'll need patience, attention, and good ingredients to make your wilderness meals into culinary masterpieces. But you'll also need to stay safe as you work with boiling liquids and hot implements.

Before you start, check for fire bans in the area, especially in drought, summer heat, and windy conditions. If possible, use an existing fire pit. Clear flammable debris in the vicinity before starting a fire, and remove any and all trip hazards nearby.

Use great caution handling or moving pots containing hot liquids. When you're not cutting something, keep your blades sheathed, closed, or put away. Watch your wardrobe, too; synthetic fabrics can melt quickly, or catch fire, should a spark hit them. Loose clothing (like long skirts or loose sleeves) is also risky around a fire.

Keep a bucket of water and shovel nearby, in case the fire gets out of control, and keep firewood upwind and away from your fire. Be extra careful while children are near the cooking fire, and never leave a cooking fire or a campfire unattended.

178 AVOID HAZARDS

Exploding stones and poisonous wood are just a few of the things to avoid when practicing the skills throughout this section. Watch out for these issues while you cook in camp.

NEVER TURN YOUR BACK ON A FIRE Fire gets hungry too, and it can burn up our dinner in the blink of an eye.

DON'T BE UNDERDONE AFTER DARK It's tricky to see the color of meat by fire light, or even with a flashlight. Deer, elk, fish, and a few others don't need extensive cooking—but everything else should be cooked thoroughly due to the risk of parasites and pathogens.

BEWARE EXPLODING ROCKS Do not use rocks from a waterway for your firepit; they may still contain moisture and can explode when heated. Wet or dry, do not use sedimentary stones like slate or shale; likewise, avoid crystalline or glassy stones like quartz or obsidian—these can also blow up in a fire.

WATCH WHAT YOU BURN Skip woods that are toxic or have a bad tasting smoke, such as yew, black locust, laurel, rhododendron, and other poisonous woods.

179 ROAST ON THE COALS

The simplest way to cook something is directly on the embers of a fire. This method inevitably results in burnt food, uneven cooking, and of course, ashes on your meal. But on the flip side, it requires no materials beyond the food and fire, except maybe a handy stick to flip the food or to remove it. Baking (and to an extent, broiling and roasting) can be done directly on the coals of a campfire. I've made tolerable steaks by dropping them on a hot bed of coals, and even made better baked potatoes and sweet potatoes with this method.

GET HOT Build a big flat bed of embers and hot ash, preferably from hardwood, before cooking. The ember bed should be several inches thick.

PUT IT IN PLACE Quick-cooking food can go in the center of the coals, where heat is highest. Foods with longer cooking times should go around the edges.

KEEP AN EYE ON IT Watch the food carefully to prevent burning, but don't turn food too often. It could end up underdone if moved too much.

180 BAKE BREAD IN THE ASHES

When I first experimented with camp breads, I naturally turned to classic outdoor texts for recipes for bannock, damper, hardtack, and every other kind of camp bread and trail biscuits you've heard of. The recipes themselves were simple enough, but the results were usually closer to ceramic than biscuit.

Then, I stumbled upon pancake mix. It turned out that the "just add water" complete pancake mix was the bread recipe that I had been hoping to find. It tastes good, and it cooks very quickly! To make an ash cake, wait for a bed of coals to become ash covered, but still very hot.

STEP 1 Mix a little water with some pancake mix, until it forms a dry dough ball. Pat it out as flat as you can, dusting your hands with dry pancake mix if the dough sticks to them.

STEP 2 Next, toss the flat cake into the bed of coals and watch it closely as it starts to fluff up. Bake it about 1 or 2 minutes on one side, depending on the heat of the coals.

STEP 3 When it becomes rigid (like a little flat biscuit), and the very bottom edge begins to brown, use a stick to flip the cake over and cook it for 30 to 60 more seconds. Use a stick to move the cooked cake out of the bed of coals, wait a few seconds for it to cool, then blow on it briskly to remove any lingering ash. Top your finished ash cake with butter, jam, honey, or maple syrup if you like, or just eat it plain and enjoy.

181 SET UP SPITS AND SKEWERS

There's something so satisfying about the process of skewering wild game meat on a wooden spit and watching it roast over a fire. But delicious doesn't happen by accident. Be sure you're using a nontoxic wood, and follow these instructions to produce tender shish kebabs and juicy roasts.

STICK WITH A SKEWER If you've roasted a marshmallow over a campfire, then you've used a skewer. This pointy stick offers a number of cooking options. For quick-cooking foods, impale the food on the sharp end and hold the skewer over the flames. For something that takes longer, set up the skewer like a dingle stick (see item 182), or prop it against a hearth rock.

STAB IT ON A SPIT You can cook bigger food items by roasting them on a wood or metal spit. If the food isn't easy to balance (like a chicken or an odd-shaped roast), make a spit with a side spike or barb of some kind to stabilize food as the spit turns.

barb

flat rock

182 PUT IT ON A STICK

Whether you are in a survival setting or just camping out with the family, you'll need a simple way to suspend your cookware over the fire to boil your water and cook your food. The dingle stick is one of the fastest rigs you can build. I can't even begin to count how many meals I've cooked using one.

STEADY ON While this is the least steady setup for holding a pot, it's secure enough when you build it right and don't overload it.

BUILD IT RIGHT Collect a straight stick, about 3 feet (1 m) long. Carve a point on the thicker end, and cut a small notch at the skinny end (or leave a natural "fork" to hold your pot handle). Stab the pointed end of the stick into the ground on an angle. Place a big stone or log under the leaning stick to prop it up. If you think you need it, place another big stone over the part of the stick in the ground, to keep it from coming up out of the dirt. Hang your pot on the end, and adjust the height of the pot by moving the support rock back and forth.

183 BUILD A GREEN-WOOD GRILL

For a real wilderness feast, the green-wood grill is a great approach. This cooking method consists of a rack of fresh live sticks or branches, set up with a fire underneath. This grill acts very much like a metal cooking grill, and you may be able to get several uses out of your sticks before they begin to burn. The grill can be supported in different ways, and you can build it to any size or shape that you like. Square, rectangular, and triangular shapes are popular, ranging in size from tiny to huge. I have built several massive grills over the years, the largest of which held enough food for 70 people.

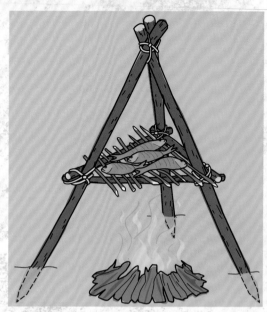

TRY A TRIPOD If you're looking for a grill with great stability, lash three crosspieces to the outside of a large tripod and then lay your greenwood rack on top of the cross members. Use vines, rawhide strips, or leather thongs to lash the crosspieces since there will be a fire nearby. Synthetic rope may melt and natural fiber rope can burn this close to the flames. If either one yields to the fire, your rack and your food will drop into the flames.

BE A SQUARE One good adaptable method of construction involves stakes or small posts that are driven into the ground to hold the rack. Cut four stakes, 1 yard (1 m) long, each with a side branch at the end. Carve a point on the end that doesn't fork, and drive these into the ground about 8 inches (20 cm). Set two stout green-wood poles in the forks, and lay a rack of green sticks perpendicular to the poles. Maintain a nice bed of coals and low flames to grill your meats and vegetables to perfection. I love roasting sweet corn this way, just as people have done here in America for centuries.

DIG A TRENCH For another option, dig a trench in the ground and lay green sticks across it. Orient the trench in the same direction as the wind, and build a fire in the bottom. This can cook your food or support a pot of water to boil. You may even be able to skip the digging, if you can find a rock crevice or narrow ditch that already exists.

184 TRY THESE GRILL TIPS

I've learned a lot about green-wood grills over the years, mostly from accidents and mistakes. Here's how to save yourself some trouble when cooking with this grill.

- Have a good bed of coals fed with hardwoods if possible.

- Watch where smoke goes and place food accordingly. Place your food in the smoke for more heat, away from it for less heat.

- Prop up flat stones against the legs of your grill to keep them from burning.

- Make a small, smoky fire to slow-cook your food and give it a great smoky flavor.

- Use green, nontoxic wood, and leave the bark on the sticks to keep the pieces from drying them out.

- Avoid woods that are sticky, like pine, spruce, and fir.

- When cooking small items, skewer several pieces together so that nothing falls through the grill.

- Don't panic when your grill sticks start to burn. Move the food away from the fire, and try to blow out the flames or squirt water on the burning sticks.

- Prop up a sagging grill with an extra forked stick or stake underneath.

- Don't let the flames reach the underside of the grill sticks. This is a sure way to light the whole rack on fire.

185 GRILL WITH A SNOWSHOE

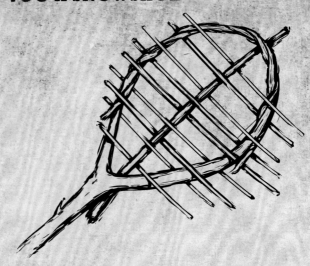

Need a little green-wood grill to cook a meal for one or two people? The "snowshoe" grill (also called a tennis-racket grill) can be used as a portable, reversible cooking surface to cook steaks, fish, and many other tasty foods. If you're careful about how close you hold it to the flames, it should last for several meals before it burns up.

STEP 1 Cut some small, straight green-wood sticks and one large forking branch. Opposite-branching woods such as maple, ash, and dogwood will give you lots of natural forks due to their opposite growth pattern. Just steer clear of buckeye and horse-chestnut wood, which look like good forks with their opposite branching, but they contain dangerous toxins. Carve a point on the end of the forked stick so that it can be stuck into the ground.

STEP 2 Bend the fork into a hoop, twisting the branch tips around each other until they hold their shape. Then lay one long straight twig down the middle of the hoop. Start out weaving shorter twigs into the hoop, with an over and under pattern. If it is tight and difficult to weave, that's good. The grill should be rigid and secure.

STEP 3 Place your food on the rack and use a couple more green sticks to pin the food into place.

STEP 4 Stab the pointed end of the grill stick into the ground. Prop the grill over the fire using rocks or a log, just as you would do if you were using a dingle stick. Turn your grill periodically, until your food is fully cooked.

Three sticks and some cordage—that's all it takes to build a tripod, your best three-legged friend in the backcountry. The finished structure is surprisingly stable, as the three legs lean inward supporting each other (as well as the occasional heavy load). Here are nine ways this contraption can help you around your bush camp.

❶ SHELTER Tipis and wickiups (brush-covered tipis) are already cone-shaped, and a natural fit with a tripod foundation. Larger, more elaborate shelters can also have a tripod at the center. Of course, the tripod has to be stout and lashed together securely, but if those conditions are met, the resulting shelter can very strong.

❷ JERKY RACK My favorite way to dry jerky is on a tripod with horizontal sticks lashed onto the sides. Even a small tripod can hold a massive amount of meat, and the best part is that it's easy to move around. As the sun tracks through the sky or the wind changes direction, you can easily move the tripod to keep it in the perfect spot.

❸ POT HANGER Just use a chain or even a wooden hook to suspend your cooking pot from the top of the tripod. If your suspension method isn't adjustable, you can adjust the three legs closer or further apart to change the height of your tripod and your hanging pot.

❹ GREEN-WOOD COOKER Build your frame from fresh-cut wood, and add a green stick rack about 20 inches (0.5 m) off the ground to create a portable green-wood cooker. This is best used over a bed of coals, as flames tend to burn these wooden frames.

❺ SMOKER A bark shell over a tripod can create a fine smoker to preserve meat, fish, or other foods. Hang food on the tripod or add a rack. Set your smoker over a small firepit containing embers from a fire and chunks of damp wood such as oak, hickory, or maple.

6 CHAIR Three sticks can act as the foundation for a comfortable camp chair. If you have a sturdy tarp or a hammock, tie on one crossbar and attach your fabric securely from the crossbar to the top of the tripod. Spread the tripod legs far apart for stability, and have a seat.

7 FIRE SHELTER Fling your poncho or a tarp over a small tripod to build a temporary shelter over the spot where you'll be building your fire. This allows you a dry place to assemble your tinder, kindling and firewood safely out of the wind, rain, sleet, and snow.

8 EMERGENCY SIGNAL A very tall tripod can be used to hoist a signal flag or some other noticeable object to act as an indicator of your distress. Hang up bright colored fabric, shiny metal, or any other high contrast item that you can spare.

9 WATER FILTER Tie three layers of cloth into a tripod, one on top of the other. Add a layer of green grass or fabric in the top layer. Then put crushed charcoal in the second layer, and sand in the bottom layer. Pour muddy or dirty water through the layers, starting at the top and collecting the water that flows out the bottom. See item 076 for more details.

186 TIE TRIPOD LASHING

There are two different ways to make a tripod. **A** For light duty tasks, you can lay the three legs side by side for lashing. **B** For heavier tasks, lay the outer poles in one direction, with the center pole the opposite way. Lash the poles and flip the center pole to line up with the outer poles, to twist the lashing and add more strength.

As for the lashing itself, lie your three poles on the ground, tie a clove hitch or square knot to one end pole, then wrap around the poles five or six times. Wrap the line twice each between the poles, working back to the original clove hitch. Finish by tying the end of the line to the free end of the starting knot. Set the legs, and your tripod is done!

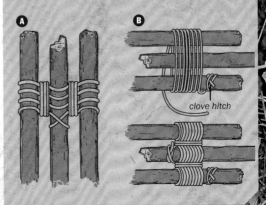

clove hitch

187 LEARN TO ROCK BOIL

If you need to boil water or make a stew and you don't happen to have a metal, glass, or clay cooking vessel, rocks will save the day. Suitable rock-boiling containers of wood, bark, and stone can allow you to safely disinfect water and cook a meal. I have even rock boiled in a hollowed-out pumpkin!

The art of rock boiling is accomplished by heating fire-friendly rocks for about 30 to 45 minutes in your campfire. Gather these from a high, dry location to minimize the chance of getting waterlogged rocks which could explode.

Once you've heated your rocks, brush or rinse off the ash, and place one or two rocks in your vessel full of water. Leave the rocks in the liquid until they stop hissing. Then replace them with new hot rocks. It will take several rocks just to bring 1 liter of water to a boil, but once it reaches boiling, fresh hot rocks will keep the liquid stewing for several minutes at a time.

TIPS Remember these tips when rock boiling.
- Use a dozen or more egg-sized to baseball-sized rocks, swapping new ones in as you go.
- Brush, blow, or rinse the ash off the hot rocks before putting them in the liquid.
- Use a partially split greenwood stick as a tongs to move the hot stones.

188 MAKE A HOT-ROCK STIR FRY

Your hot rocks can help you cook up more than soup or stew, to expand your dining options.

STEP 1 Heat several egg-sized stones for 20 minutes in your campfire. While these stones heat up, chop some wild vegetables and game meat into small pieces.

STEP 2 Place the food in a large wooden bowl or a bark container, adding a small amount of oil or a few gobs of raw animal fat. Add a little water too, in order to create steam for faster and more even cooking.

STEP 3 Pick a rock out of the fire with tongs, blow off any ash, and place it into the bowl of raw food. Stir the mixture slowly with a stick. The food will begin to cook from the heat of the rock. Once a cooking stone has cooled and is no longer sizzling, replace it with another hot stone from the fire.

STEP 4 Continue to stir hot stones through the food until all of the meat has changed color and is cooked through. Serve with one stone left in the bowl, to keep the food hot.

189 SET UP A ROCK FRYING PAN

Frying is a delicious way to go in primitive cooking. The crispy edges and caramelization that frying can create are mouth-watering. As a testament to the quality of this ancient cooking method, rock frying is still being used in modern times across the world.

GO ROCK HUNTING To get started on your own culinary adventure of rock cooking, you'll need a flat or concave stone about an inch thick. Avoid sandstone and other rough-surfaced stones that food will stick to, making frying difficult. You'll also want to skip any stones collected near the water as well as flat slabs of slate and shale, all of which tend to explode when heated.

BUILD YOUR PAN Once you've picked your stone, set it up securely with about a foot (30 cm) of clearance from the ground. If the rock is too low, you cannot maintain a decent fire underneath. Prop your rock pan on top of other rocks, or over a trench in the ground with the fire underneath.

TRY SOME STAKES One method of getting some height is to drive three green-wood stakes into the ground and set the flat rock on top. You'll want to stand up three flat stones underneath the frying rock to protect the green sticks from burning.

LEVEL UP To make sure your pan is level, pour a little water into the center of the rock. The water will run off the low side of the pan, so you can slip small stone chips under the low side of the rock frying pan to level it up.

When you're ready to cook, build a big enough fire under the rock so that the flames are touching the underside of the rock, or even curling up around the edges of the frying rock. Maintain a coal bed under your griddle, and feed it plenty of twigs and split sticks.

TIPS Keep these pointers in mind when making your own rock frying pan.
- Maintain the flames for effective frying.
- Choose a rock with a slight depression.
- Don't get too attached to your rock frying pan, as the heat will probably break it eventually.

190 GIVE BIG ANIMALS A BOOST

When you have to cook a whole animal in a hurry, it's hard to get the inside done without burning the outside. It's also hard to achieve well-done meat in a small steam pit or a hastily fired stone oven. But what if you could add a little more heat to the equation? One of my backwoods cooking tricks is to heat up a stone for 15 to 20 minutes in a fire, and insert it into the body

This is a great source of supplemental heat, and it's easy to do. Shove a hot rock up inside a wild turkey before you drop it into a steam pit. Place a hot rock inside the ribs of a raccoon in your rock oven. This extra heat not only gives you a faster cooking time, but it gives you a greater margin of food safety too. Just don't make the stone too hot, or the direct contact will burn

191 BUILD A STONE OVEN

Once built, a stone oven can be used over and over by simply building up the fire inside again. This internally fired oven is usually made of very large stones that can absorb a lot of heat, hold it, and radiate it back for some time. It works because the fire's heat builds up in the stones and then radiates back out for even, consistent cooking.

START WITH STONE Choose a large piece of a stone or several pieces to become the floor of the oven, or look for an existing flat stone in the ground for an oven base. Pick out some blocky chunks for the walls and plenty of little pieces to fill gaps. Select a flat rock to act as a door and a big rock to act as the top of the oven.

MAKE SOME MORTAR Dig some local clay or mud, and start building. Lay out your oven floor rocks, and build the walls around them. Find the best spot for each rock, and use mud mortar and little stone pieces to secure each rock and fill gaps. Lay the big rock over the top as a lid, and fit the door for a snug seal. Leave a gap in the back of the oven, just under the lid, to act as a chimney, and find a rock that plugs the hole to keep more heat inside while cooking. Don't worry if it doesn't look like a brick pizza oven. Just about any tight pile of durable rocks with a hole in the middle can be a workable oven.

FIRE IT UP Burn your fire inside the oven for at least an hour and a half; 2 hours would be better. Keep the door propped up to the side to absorb heat, and the chimney open. Once it's hot enough, quickly scoop out the embers and ash, place your food inside, and seal the door and chimney (using more mud if needed). Allow the food to bake for its typical baking time, plus a little extra—up to 1 hour. After that, the oven will have cooled enough that it's no longer baking; it's just keeping food warm. I have made tender, juicy roasts and sweet desserts in the deep woods with this type of oven.

192 BAKE LIKE A CHAMP

Externally fired baking ovens are usually made of thinner stone (like stone slabs), and the fire is maintained all the way around the outside of the cooking box. These ovens are very versatile, and you can place the food inside before, during, or after the firing. Here's how to put one together.

BEGIN BUILDING Collect rocks that can handle high heat. Set up a group of stones to act as pillars to support a large flat rock which will be the floor of the oven. You can also use a rock frying setup as the base of your oven. To make a typical square oven shape, build three walls atop the flat rock.

FILL THE GAPS When caulking stone ovens, you can harvest clay from creeks and riverbanks, or by digging down to the clay level in areas that have clay-rich soil. Clay comes in many colors and textures, but good clay should be able to be rolled into a "rope" and tied like a pretzel without breaking.

FINISH IT OFF Cover the top of the oven with one or several large, wide rocks to form the lid of the oven. Caulk every gap with clay to seal up the box. Select a good door and make sure it fits. You don't need an opening to act as a chimney; the flat rock for your door will be the only opening. Once built, you can fire the oven right away, or wait for the clay to dry.

193 COOK IN A CLAY POT

You can make an excellent oven by covering a traditional clay pot with hot coals. Squab or small game birds are delicious when prepared this way, and they fit nicely on a short, fat stake driven into the ground.

STEP 1 Stab a green-wood stake into the ground next to your campfire. Impale a roast, a small hen, or some veggies on the stake and cover it with an upturned clay pot.

STEP 2 Move some of the coals from the nearby fire to surround the pot. Continue to bury the pot in hot coals until it has been mostly covered. As the coals burn down, replace them every 15 to 20 minutes.

STEP 3 After about an hour or two of tending your clay-pot oven, carefully remove it to check on the food. When vegetables are soft and meat is falling from the bone, it's done.

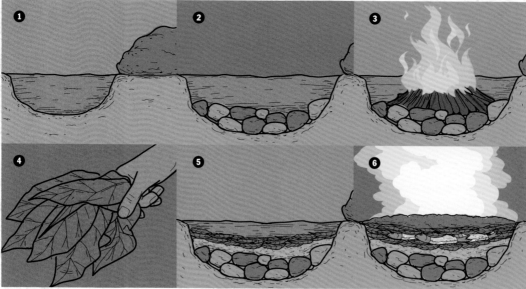

This elaborate cooking method is used around the world, often for feasts and special occasions. It's worth the trouble, because it makes great-tasting food that stays hot for hours until you're ready to eat. A steam pit is a hole in the ground (or raised mound) with hot rocks at the bottom, covered in dirt or sand. Wrapped food is sandwiched between two layers of green vegetation atop the sand. The pile is covered with dirt and/or tarps to hold steam.

STEP 1 Dig a pit, or collect loose soil or sand to make a mound. The pit can be as small as 18 inches (0.5 m) deep and wide, or as big as you have rocks and food to fill it with, and about 3 feet (1 m) deep. Any shape will work.

STEP 2 Collect a pile of local rocks that can take a lot of heat. Make sure you have enough to fill the bottom of the pit; ideally you can place them in there like a puzzle to see where the stones fit best.

STEP 3 You now have a choice now of leaving the stones in the pit and building the fire on top of them or taking the rocks out of the pit and placing them in a big fire. Either way, the stones should be heated for 2 hours. If you heat the rocks in the pit, scoop the remaining wood, charcoal, coals, and ash out of the pit when the rocks are hot enough. If you heat the stones outside the pit, use a shovel or a large green-wood pole to roll or push the rocks into the pit.

STEP 4 You can also gather your green vegetation during the 2-hour rock-firing time. Good steam-pit vegetation can be green grass, seaweed, pine boughs full of green needles, and any other abundant nontoxic green plant material.

STEP 5 Once the pit has nothing but hot rocks in it, apply about 8 inches (10 cm) of damp soil or sand to insulate the stones. Add 8 to 12 inches (20 to 30 cm) of green vegetation, then place your food in a single layer on top of the vegetation. Root vegetables are great when cooked like this, and so is seafood. Wrap tender foods that fall apart (like fish) with large edible leaves (like burdock).

STEP 6 Bury the food with your remaining vegetation. Cover it with a tarp and soil, or just plain soil. Come back three or more hours later, dig up your food, and enjoy. The food will stay hot for several hours.

195 MOUND UP A MEAL

A bountiful coastal area provides delectable wild foods. From clams and lobsters to edible seaweeds and crabs, all of these tasty foods provide us with great nutrition, and the beach provides us with all the necessary materials to cook them. Rather than digging a pit to cook, we can create a steam mound. The beach gives us all the food, sand, and seaweed—and even firewood.

STEP 1 Gather some rocks from a dry location (not on the beach). Start by firing your dry rocks for about 2 hours.

STEP 2 Gather your edibles and seaweed. If you are familiar with local species of edible seaweed, add it to the harvest. Otherwise, grab what's available to surround your food in the mound. A tarp will help tremendously.

STEP 3 Using a stick, roll or slide your hot rocks out of the fire to make a platform. Quickly cover this with several inches (5 to 10 cm) of damp sand. Add a similar layer of seaweed and place your food on top in one layer. Cover this with more seaweed to insulate the mound; if you have a tarp, drape it over the top to keep the sand from sifting through. Heap up sand over the entire mound to seal in the heat and the steam. Let it cook for at least 2 hours; three would be better. When you feel that enough time has passed, carefully start removing the sand from the top of the mound and lift out some of the seaweed. Be careful—this should be very hot. Uncover your food and enjoy it!

196 BUILD A BAMBOO STEAMER

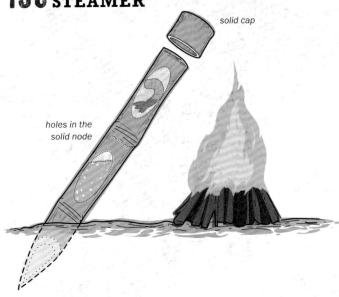

solid cap

holes in the solid node

If you have access to bamboo, you can make a great bushcraft steamer to cook plant and animal foods.

STEP 1 Using a machete or similar tool, chop a green section from the biggest bamboo stalk available. It needs to have two nodes (solid sections) intact.

STEP 2 Cut a point on one end, and leave the other end square. Cut another section from lower down on the same bamboo plant, with one node intact to make a cap. This will be placed over the end of the steamer. It shouldn't be a tight fit, since the steam could make it pop off like a projectile.

STEP 3 Now comes the tricky part! With a long hardwood spike and a rock hammer, pierce a few holes in the upper node of your steamer. You don't want to break the node out or crack the bamboo, just make a few holes for water and steam to escape.

STEP 4 With the holes in place, pour water down into the tube to load up most of the space in the lower section of bamboo, and load your food into the upper section. Add your end piece and stick the stalk into the ground next to your fire. As the heat begins to transfer through the wall of the bamboo, it will turn the water to steam, which will rise up through the food. This will cook the food slowly and gently.

197 DIG AN EARTH OVEN

This might be the most complicated primitive cooking setup, but it's also the most versatile. The earth oven is a round fire pit connected to a trench in the ground. A stone cooking box spans the trench and a mound of earth covers much of the box. The trench ends with a chimney, which rises up through the dirt mound to create a better draft for the fire pit. You can cook over an open fire in the pit, bake or rock fry in the stone oven, and cook over the mouth of the chimney like a stove top at home. You'll need a shovel or digging stick to excavate the pit and trench, and an assortment of rocks, but that's about all you'll need to make this marvelous multiuse cooking appliance.

STEP 1 Lay out the pit and trench in the ground where you'll build the oven. The pit should be dug about 1 foot (30 cm) deep and about 2 feet (60 cm) across. The trench should connect to this hole, the same depth into the ground and about 10 inches (25 cm) wide. The length of the trench will vary, but I usually make mine about 2 feet (60 cm) long. If possible, orient the oven so prevailing winds hit the fire pit and travel down the trench.

STEP 2 Place a flat rectangular stone slab over the trench, near the edge of the fire pit, for a frying surface and the floor of the oven. Build up two side walls and a rear wall from chunks of stone and place a large flat stone over the top for a lid.

STEP 3 Next, build a chimney out of stone or mud. Use the back wall of the oven box as part of the chimney to make it more stable and to conduct more heat to the oven, then bury the oven box and chimney in dirt. I'll often place three pyramidal stones around the chimney top, so I can set a pot, pan, or griddle over the chimney without blocking the airflow.

STEP 4 Start a fire in the fire pit, push some coals down into the trench, then add sticks for more flames. Smoke should issue from the chimney as the oven box is heated by both the radiant heat of the fire pit, and the conducted heat of the oven box floor and rear wall. When it's hot enough, place your food in the oven, over the chimney, or in the fire pit to cook.

198 PICK THE BEST FOODS

There have been some epic feasts in my camp, and some legendary flops, when working with the steam pit. Root vegetables are usually excellent when pulled from the pit and buttered while hot. Other things are not so tasty. Since you are cooking in the soil, there is always an earthiness to the flavor of the foods—and this isn't always a good match. Once I prepared a steam pit for a winter survival class years ago. The only green vegetation available then was pine needle; the skinless pork loin we cooked among them ended up pine flavored and tough as a dog's rubber chew toy. To spare you unpleasantness of this sort, here are some of the best foods to drop into a steam pit.

ROOT VEGETABLES Potatoes, carrots, turnips, and wild edible roots and such are already earthy in taste, so you won't notice the "pit" flavor at all!

SWEET POTATOES Drizzle maple syrup over a pot of yams or sweet potatoes, cover with a lid, and place it in the pit to cook into gooey ambrosia!

EGGS Store bought or stolen from a nest, eggs are a delight from the steam pit. The yolk center may still be creamy soft if you don't cook it too long.

FISH AND FOWL Cooking fish and birds by steaming keeps them tender, and the skin holds out any other flavors.

GREENS Plenty of strong-flavored greens can hold their own in a pit, keeping their taste once cooked.

199 WORK WITH WILD SEASONINGS

Many people are surprised to discover that there's a wild counterpart to each herb and spice that we use today. Through centuries of selective breeding, we have changed and modified many species of seasoning plants, but they are still similar to their wild progenitors. If we are lucky enough to find and identify a wild forebear of a familiar spice, then we can use it in our cooking. Use a plant ID guide to make sure you have the right plant. What follows is a list of common wild plants that can spice up your food.

WILD ONION Dozens of species of wild onion and garlic are found worldwide, and are an excellent replacement for cultivated varieties. Use the bulb or tops, fresh or dried, to add an oniony flavor to anything. Make sure it's the genuine article, and not a dangerous look-a-like.

PEPPERGRASSES Shepherd's purse, cow cress, and other "peppergrasses" are actually part of the mustard family. The green seedpods and dried seeds have a peppery flavor.

SORREL Several sour wild edible plants have the word "sorrel" in their name. Wood sorrel have sets of three heart-shaped leaves and other sorrels like the sheep sorrel have little shear-head-shaped leaves. Their sour flavor comes from oxalic acid, and can substitute for lemon.

SASSAFRAS The dried leaves of sassafras impart a citrus flavor to soups and stews, and act as a thickener. This tree has long been a secret ingredient in gumbo and other southern recipes.

200 USE A DUTCH OVEN

For hundreds of years these wide cast-iron pots have been some the most versatile cooking implements available. They can perform like a pot to boil water and cook stews. They can act as a griddle or pan, by frying in the lid or the oven bottom. And they can also act like an oven, baking everything from bread and cakes to cookies. The only drawbacks can be the weight and the price, as Dutch ovens can be both heavy and expensive.

BAKING To bake in the Dutch oven, build up a large bed of coals in a fire. Set the oven into the coals and place coals on top of the lid. Try to follow the average cooking times for the food you are preparing, and replace the coals on top of the lid as they burn down.

BOILING You'll need flames underneath the oven to boil successfully. The attached bail (handle) can be hung from a chain, dangling from a tripod or tree limb. You could also thread a green-wood pole through the bail and support the pole with posts or convenient forks in small trees.

201 BUILD A COOKING CRANE

When fireplaces cooked meals in the home, swinging pot cranes let a cook move heavy pots with greater safety. We can adopt this technique for our camp by building simple cooking cranes. Here are two ways to do it beside your campfire.

❶ CARVE A THREE-STICK CRANE One long stick, a forked stick, and a hooked stick can create a very effective cooking crane over your fire. Cut two pieces of wood with side branches. One should be "right side up" for the fork, and the other should be turned "upside down" to make the hook (since branches don't usually grow downward). Carve points on the ends of these stakes and drive them into the ground. The upward fork should be closer to the fire, and the downward hook farther away. Place the long pole in this rig, and leverage will hold it in place. This setup is good for small pots, but not sturdy enough bigger vessels.

❷ MAKE A MEGA CRANE For bigger pots, you'll need a bigger crane. Select a log with a sturdy side branch. Chop a sharp point on the end of the log with a hatchet or machete. Using a large rock for a hammer, drive it into the ground beside your fire pit. Drive in two smaller support stakes on the side toward the fire. Twist the log until it spins well enough in the dirt to be able to spin while holding a heavy pot. Carve or saw a shallow notch in the end of the branch to hold the pot handle, prop up a flat rock to protect the base of the crane from the fire, and your crane is ready to use.

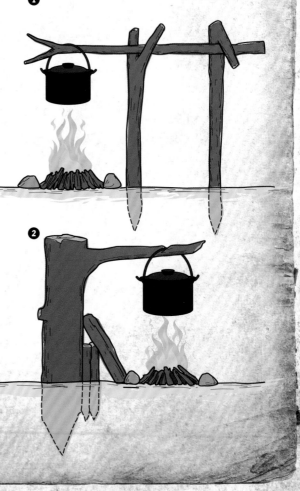

The reflecting oven is another venerable cooking appliance, at the least dating back to colonial America. These simple ovens catch the heat of a fire and focus it into a central baking area. In use for centuries, the reflectors can be any size, virtually any shape, and made from almost any new or cast-off sheet metal (or even flat slabs of stone). Here's how to make a metal one with some tin snips and a little ingenuity (and we recommend some leather gloves, too).

GATHER YOUR SUPPLIES For its basic incarnation, you will need some sheet metal, some snips to cut it, and a pan or grill to place inside the unit. For the one that's pictured here, I "borrowed" an old bread pan from the kitchen (please don't tell my missus about that). For larger and heavier units, I'd definitely recommend a drill and some pop rivets to secure the joints, or sheet-metal screws—whichever you prefer.

MAKE YOUR SHAPES A simple wedge-shaped reflector oven is the easiest to build. Fold a large rectangular piece of sheet metal in half to create the main piece. Then cut out some 90-degree triangles to build the sides. If you're good with sheet metal and have some specialized tools for it, this entire project will be a breeze. I just used the snips and my gloved hands, and cut some interlocking tabs to join the two triangles to the main piece.

SET IT UP The final bit is the easiest: just set it all up. I used several stones behind the unit to make it stand up by the fire (though integrated legs are better). I also used stones in the front to support the pan. More traditional setups involve holes in the side panels which allow you to use spits and skewers, and to place rods that would support a pan or grill. However you build it, just make sure that it is sturdy and able to stand up to the weight of the food—and the likelihood of being bumped by the cook.

MAINTAIN YOUR COALS AND COOK! A large bed of coals is just what you need for baking in the reflector oven. Build up a large fire, allow it to go to coals, and then set your oven right next to it. You can use both coals and flames when cooking forgiving foods like a roast on a spit.

203 TRY THESE COOKING TIPS

You may be a master chef in your home kitchen (or even in a restaurant kitchen), but things will be quite different when you're cooking over an open fire. Without the help of all your favorite equipment and push-button temperature controls, you may think it's hopeless to try to create a gourmet meal, but that's just not true. Nature gives us everything we need to succeed, if we work within the limitations of the materials and the techniques. And these tips won't hurt at all, either.

CHOOSE YOUR WOOD Hardwoods are usually the best firewoods. A bed of hardwood coals will keep a fire burning steadily.

KEEP IT ON HAND Have your firewood gathered and ready before you start cooking, or have someone collecting wood for you, so you can watch the fire and food. Split wood burns better than whole chunks. It's best to remove bark before burning (as it's not that flammable) and split your firewood into smaller sections.

KNOW THE DIFFERENCE Flames are needed to boil and fry food; coals are used to roast, bake, and broil food.

WATCH THE HEAT Food is much less likely to burn at gradually decreasing temperatures. Food is much more likely to burn at gradually or sharply increasing temperatures (so don't get impatient near the end of the cook time and stoke up the fire to a blaze; you'll burn your meal).

COOK PROPERLY Be sure you know which foods have pathogens and parasites, and that need to be cooked all the way through. Make sure that food is cooked in such a way to kill dangerous bacteria on the surface or mixed up in food.

204 FRY IN A PAN

Your camp frying pan can be a cast-iron beauty, your stainless-steel pan from home, or a reproduction of an old-fashioned pan meant to hang over the fire like a cook pot. Keep these tips in mind when using a fry pan in your bushcraft camp.

STAY HOT You'll need flames to effectively fry foods, so keep a pile of dry twigs or split kindling available to perk up sluggish fires.

CONTROL THE FLAME You're most likely to experience a grease fire while frying oily foods over a hot fire. Keep the heat manageable and keep something nearby to cover a flaming pan. Never throw water or flour on a grease fire, as the results can be explosive.

BUTTER UP Greasy foods like bacon and sausage provide their own oil for the frying pan, but other foods (like eggs and pancakes) will need oil or butter to prevent sticking.

SAVOR THE FLAVOR If you've got some tasty grease in the pan (like bacon fat), leave it in there if you're planning to fry something else. Meats and vegetables are delicious when fried in bacon fat or sausage grease.

SAVE DISHES Let your pan cool a bit, and then you can eat right out of the frying pan like a plate. You'll have one less dish to wash, and the metal will keep your food warm.

205 TEST A CAST-IRON GRIDDLE

Rectangular cast-iron griddles are a wonderful cooking implement. These heavy flat pieces of iron can serve up breakfast, lunch, and dinner. The griddle can be propped on a pair of stone blocks, or even rest on a convenient pair of logs. Level it with little flat stones to keep any cooking oil from running off, and make sure there is enough clearance underneath the griddle to maintain your fire.

Like all cast-iron ware, griddles need to be seasoned to limit the food from sticking. To do this in the field, fry some bacon using the cookware. Wipe the grease all over the cooking surface and keep it near the heat for half an hour. Wipe off the excess grease and store the cast iron in a dry place. Never use soap on seasoned cast iron.

206 DRY IT— YOU'LL LIKE IT

It's a happy problem to have more food than you can eat, but it's still a problem. Thankfully, drying your surplus food needs no special gear. Dried meat and plant foods can last for a very long time, since the lack of moisture is an inhospitable environment for the organisms that cause decay. Here's how to preserve both meat and plants.

DRY YOUR JERKY Start with fresh raw meat. Cooked meat that is dried can lead to food poisoning. Slice the meat thin and across the grain. Cut your pieces less than ¼ inch (0.5 cm) thick and cut perpendicular to the grain of the meat. Trim off all visible fat, or it will go rancid; fat must be preserved by rendering, a whole different process from jerky making. While the meat is still juicy, sprinkle on salt, sugar, or spices. These are optional, but salt creates a less hospitable environment for bacteria. Hang your jerky slices on a rack or on twigs and branches around camp. Don't leave it unattended, or birds and other thieves will get it. Jerky can be dried near a small smoky fire to add smoke flavoring and keep flies away while the meat dries. Don't dry the jerky over the fire or it will cook, and go bad in days. Depending on the humidity, the jerky may dry in one day or several days. Don't leave it out overnight for the damp and the critters. Put it somewhere dry instead. Flip it a few times during the drying process. When it becomes slightly brittle, it is done.

DESICCATE FRUITS AND VEGGIES In a similar process to jerky making, fruits and vegetables can be dried for long-term storage. And since so many plant foods are seasonal, this may be the only way to enjoy them "out of season." To get started drying, slice fruits and bulky vegetables into thin pieces. Cut berries and small fruits in half. Remove seeds when practical (you'll never get them out of blueberries or blackberries). Dry the small food pieces in the sun for a day or more. Dry larger pieces for several days, until they don't seem to change anymore. Bring your plant foods in each night to avoid dampness and animal thieves, and bring them in during damp weather.

207 GET SMOKED

Smoke has been used for ages to preserve many natural materials. From tanned deer skins to food, the cocktail of chemicals in smoke will discourage the growth of bacteria and fungi—the chief troublemakers for spoilage. There are two main methods: hot and cold smoking.

CHOOSE YOUR METHOD Hot smoking involves a closed area to hold in the smoke and the heat from your smoke materials. Food is cooked and permeated with a smoky flavor. Meat and fish will last for a week or more, depending on the temperature. Cold smoking is done at cooler temperatures, for a longer time. This is more of a drying than cooking process. Cold smoked foods may last for months. Both hot and cold smoking should take place in some kind of sealed environment, though you can achieve smoked items with a smudge fire (one with no flames) underneath the items in the open air (but not on a windy day).

GET THE WOOD A smudge can be made from a pile of hardwood coals, with damp wood chips over the top. Applewood makes a great, sweet smoke perfect for poultry and pork. Hickory gives a rich, sharp flavor and makes hot long-burning coals. Maple wood chips are another excellent choice, especially for cheeses. Mesquite is coveted for its earthy flavor. Ash is a light-flavored smoke, great with fish and poultry. Red oak is good on ribs and pork, while white oak makes long-lasting coals. Avoid toxic species such as black locust, yew, buckeye, horse chestnut, rhododendron, and mountain laurel; or bitter resinous woods: cedar, cypress, redwood, fir, pine, spruce, or other needle-bearing trees.

208 BUILD AN ICE CACHE

The winter air can be our nemesis if we are stuck in the cold, but can also be used to our advantage. If you get caught without power, you can place your frozen food in a cooler full of ice and set the cooler outside in a shady area or an unheated shed. Or you can do what our ancestors did by freezing it in an outdoor ice cache.

PICK THE BEST SPOT The ideal spot for an ice cache is near your dwelling and on the north side of a large structure. This northern orientation will keep the southerly sun from warming up that spot during the day, and in the shade, your ice will last longer. Stone-age peoples made ice caches in pits dug on the north side of boulder outcroppings, to provide shade to preserve the ice and a marker to find the spot again, even in a snowy landscape.

BUILD YOUR BOX Lay out ice blocks to create a small ice platform. Your food will sit on this, rather than the bare ground. Then, using blocks of uniform thickness, build a wall around the foundation. Carve or saw the ice to make each block fit tightly. If you need something to act as "chinking" to fill any gaps, apply slush while the air is subfreezing. The slush will freeze and fill the gap. Finally, make a slab of ice that will cover the entire structure like a lid. Check the lid for fit, load in your food, and seal the lid on there.

HAVE A SECURITY PLAN Hungry scavengers will be very interested in your cache—some critters can even smell it through the ice. Most won't get to it, but for extra security, bury the ice box in slushy snow and let it freeze into a solid block. Humans with tools can break the ice and retrieve the food. If animals keep visiting the box, you could also set up traps to take advantage of the situation.

209 MAKE PEMMICAN

An ancient forebear of modern survival rations, pemmican was originally made by North American Indians as a traveling food and cold-weather snack. It's made by pounding dried meat into a powder, then blending it with warm animal fat. Dried fruits, berries, or other foods may be added. This mixture can be rolled into balls, pressed into a loaf, or formed into cakes. To eat it, simply pop a piece in your mouth or add it to a pot of boiling water to make a high-calorie soup base.

YOU'LL NEED:
· 8 ounces (0.2 kg) lard
· An 8-ounce (0.2-kg) cup packed tight with powdered jerky
· 8 ounces (0.2 kg) dried fruit
· Optional: flour, sugar, salt, spices

PREP FOR SUCCESS The lard, jerky, and fruit are essential ingredients. Some folks add a little bit of flour for extra carbs, or a handful of salt, sugar, or spices to make this mess taste a little better. Keep an eye on the mixture's temperature—cold lard won't incorporate well with the other ingredients, and melted lard will cook the jerky slightly, leading to dangerous spoilage. Get the lard to a soft state, below 100°F (38°C), by warming it slightly or stirring it aggressively.

BLEND AND STORE Add the lard to a bowl containing all the other ingredients and stir until well incorporated (about 2 minutes). Loosely wrap the pemmican in wax paper, and store it in a cool, dry, dark place. It can last for months before the fat turns rancid, especially in cold weather. Just make sure to store it out of the reach of pests, too. Once you get used to the odd feeling of grease running down the back of your throat as you chew, you just might start to enjoy this superfood.

CONTAINERS

What a pain it would be to go without containers in the wild! How would you hike with no backpack to hold your gear or bottle to hold your drinking water? How to transport food or store it without spoilage? Baskets, bags, bowls, buckets, and bindles have been essential throughout history for the transport, preparation, and storage of supplies. Learn the following skills and you'll never lack for a container in the wild.

210 PICK A BASKET

The diversity of cultures weaving baskets and the variety of materials across the globe have led to a mind-boggling number of basketry styles and weaving patterns. For simplicity, let's look at the four major styles of basketry that we could easily produce in the wilderness.

WICKER The term "wicker" covers a broad style of basketry that typically involves the use of vines, roots, and other sorts of round, flexible materials. Long materials are used as "weavers" to go over and under the "spokes" coming from the basket's center or base. An incredible diversity of basket shapes, materials, and patterns are seen throughout the world's wicker basketry.

COIL Another type of basketry uses a spiral "coil" of material and some flexible binding to weave a spiral-constructed basket. As with wicker, an incredibly diverse number of materials can be used, with great variations on the stitching used to hold it all together. The shapes of the finished baskets all tend to be rounded, due to the coiling construction methods used to build them.

BARK Technically, bark containers are not true baskets, as they are not woven. Bark baskets are a simple group of containers based on a few major patterns of cutting, folding, and stitching flexible bark sheets and pieces to produce a wide variety of container shapes and sizes. Many different types have been made throughout the world, from cooking containers to canoes.

SPLINT Wooden splint and bark-strip splint baskets are a type of basketry that uses a checkerboard pattern on the base, with an over-under weave that circles around the basket. These baskets are very similar to some wicker styles in the way that all of the separate pieces are woven together.

211 WEAVE A BASKET

There are plenty of materials you can use to make a coil basket. For the core, you could use grasses, vines, long leaves, bark fibers, cordage material, roots, slender branches, and woody shoots. Ideally, the core materials should be dead and dry to minimize shrinkage and loosening. The binding materials can be flexible split roots, vines, cordage, string, strips of flexible bark, or long leaves. You'll also want to have a hollow tube to act as a sizing gauge for your core material and a large needle to move the binding through the walls

STEP 1 Start by wrapping a tapered bundle of core material.

STEP 2 Curl the tapered bundle into a circle, and wrap the bundle around the circle.

STEP 3 Stitch your outer coil to the neighboring inner coil, and begin working outward.

STEP 4 Slide a bone or bamboo tube down over the core material to hold it together while you work

STEP 5 Tie knots in the cord to lengthen it when needed, and feed more material every few wraps to keep the core the same diameter through the basket.

STEP 6 Pull the coil upward when you're ready to make the sides of the basket, and continue stitching.

STEP 7 When you're ready to finish the basket, let the bundle taper to finish the rim.

STEP 8 Push the needle back through the rim and snip it off to finish. Enjoy your new basket!

212 CHOP A BOWL

A wooden bowl isn't just some rustic decoration to put on a shelf. Wooden bowls allow you to carry water, and even boil it by adding hot stones to the bowl. You can eat out of your bowl and use it for storage.

Your trusty hatchet can help you get your bowl started. Yes, it does a rough job, but you can chop out a quick cavity in a chunk of softwood quite easily using this technique.

Once you've done the basic shaping work you can finish it off using one of the techniques described in the following pages.

GET CHOPPING Start in the center of the wood, making small chops on a 45-degree angle and moving the wood in a circle. Keep chopping to remove chips of wood until you reach the desired cavity size. Watch those thumbs, and don't get sloppy.

DON'T BREAK IT Leave the walls of the bowl several inches thick. You'll also want to avoid that one final perfectionist chop, which tends to just split the bowl in half instead.

213 CARVE A BOWL

The hook knife (aka crooked knife) is an odd tool, and an old one. Today, farriers use a dull version of this blade to clean the underside of horse hooves, but other than that, these tools aren't seen much anymore. Yet in times gone by, these knives were more common and often used to carve wooden bowls, spoons, ladles, and other necessities.

BEND A KNIFE A crooked knife is just that: a blade curved into a hook-shaped tool. With it, you can "scoop" shavings of wood from a chunk and hollow out a bowl. You can bend a knife made from soft steel with a bit of campfire heating and rock hammering (just like the earliest blacksmiths did). You'll just need to re-harden it before using the blade.

PICK YOUR WOOD To carve your first bowl, start with a softwood chunk like cedar or basswood, or any local softwoods that aren't prone to

215 CHOOSE WISELY

For carved bowls and utensils, you can get away with using live or dead wood, but for coal-burned articles, you'll want to be more selective.

Choose wood that is dry, rot-free, and from a nontoxic wood species (especially if you will be using it to hold food). Softwoods are fine choices for coal-burned articles, and they are able to burn out faster than hardwoods. Hardwoods make more durable items, however. Sycamore is well known for being a durable wooden bowl. Some woods, like tulip poplar, are fine for short-term use, but they tend to "check" (split) more than others over time, or when exposed to cycles of heat, moisture, and drying.

Avoid woods that can have toxicity, such as black locust, yew, buckeye, horse chestnut, rhododendron, and laurel, for spoons or food vessels. It is possible that these woods could impart toxins into food and drink.

216 FINISH THE JOB

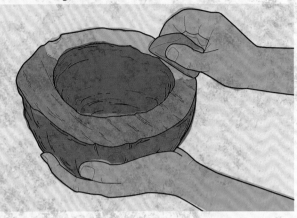

After creating your wooden item, it is perfectly usable, but it will last longer and can be more pleasant to use if you finish the wood surface to protect and preserve the item.

SAND AWAY Start polishing the item with sandpaper, a round cobble of sandstone, or a sprinkle of actual sand and a coarse stone, for a finished look and feel to the wood.

BURNISH IT Another step you can take is burnishing: a polishing technique which involves rubbing a hard, smooth object on wood to make its surface harder, more durable, and less permeable. Burnishing can be done with a metal spoon, a smooth deer antler point, or a glassy river rock. After burnishing (or instead), a final finish of edible nut oil or rendered animal fat can be rubbed onto the wood to seal the surface. This adds a slight waterproofing and lends a little more shine.

CAVEMAN'S CORNER

217 HACK OUT A HOLLOW

You can still make a wooden vessel if you don't have a fire to burn a cavity or metal tools to cut into the wood. Take a page from our distant forebears and use a stone hand axe to chop out the side of a soft rotten log. This trough will be a rough and chunky basin, but it will catch rainwater and hold dry materials until you can make something more durable and more portable.

218 GET TO KNOW SOAPSTONE

Soapstone (also called steatite) is found worldwide; before the discovery of ceramics, our ancestors used it to make fireproof bowls and cooking pots.

Soapstone is soft enough to be easily shaped, yet it is still dense and durable. It is nonabsorbent, acid-proof, unaffected by extreme temperatures, and very resistant to thermal shock. No other natural stone can be worked in the same set of ways (sanding, carving, sawing, or scraping) and hold the same sharp shapes, smooth surfaces, and fine details. The colors of this stone vary greatly, from black to white, with an entire rainbow of colors in between, which become even deeper and richer when the object is sealed with hot wax or oil.

Soapstone is so soft that you can identify it just by scratching a piece with bone or soft stone; the resulting dust that is scratched off will have a slick, soapy, or greasy feel (hence the name soapstone).

Look for soapstone in areas where limestone and other sedimentary stones occur. Your best chances to find it are usually along waterways where most of the local stones are exposed, washed, and on display for your selection.

Just so you know, soapstone can contain naturally occurring asbestos; however, this is not believed to be harmful in the same way that refined asbestos can be. Either way, work this stone outdoors and remove any dusty clothing before coming indoors.

219 SHAPE SOAPSTONE

You can carve soapstone with simple unmodified stone tools, but you'll get better results with specialized implements.

Ⓐ TRY A CHISEL For millennia, people have used hard stone chisels to shape soapstone vessels; bone chisels can also bite into it. A Native American style of bone chisel works best for me—a deer leg bone cut to a point, with four teeth sawed into the working end. The chisel is held at a very shallow angle and tapped with a wooden mallet to cut through the soapstone.

Ⓑ WORK WITH STONE Other useful tools include stone hand axes and adzes for chopping, and rough stone slabs and rounded cobble sanders for smoothing. Work the exterior in any direction, with greater care shown to thin areas and edges. The interior should only be worked from the rim toward the center, to reduce risk of breaking a chunk out of the side. As with a wooden bowl, sand the surfaces to finish the item, with successively finer sanding materials.

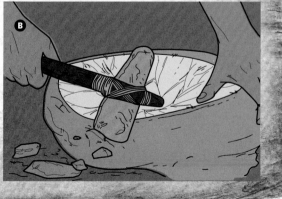

220 MAKE A CLAY POT

The knowledge to turn mud into pottery was a major leap forward for prehistoric cultures until the development of metal pots. Clay is lighter than soapstone, easier to transport, heats up faster, and can be made into much larger pots.

GATHER CLAY The first part of making a pot is harvesting clay from creek and riverbanks, or by digging down in the ground to a clay layer in areas that have clay-rich soil. Clay comes in many colors, from white to red to dark gray. It can also have different textures, if sand and small bits of stone are blended in. But all good pottery clay should be able to get tied in a knot. Roll the wet clay into a "rope" shape and tie a knot in it (like a pretzel). If it doesn't break, it's a good candidate. Clay can be harvested fresh and wet, right out of the ground, or collected dry in more arid climates. Grind your dry clay into powder and add a little water to rehydrate it. Mix in sand or stone dust to "temper" the clay. Add one part sand or crushed quartz to two parts clay (temper should be ⅓ the volume), and the mix should be ready.

BUILD A POT Your first project can be a bowl or very small pot. Shape a concave vessel from your clay mix, smoothing and compressing it as you go. Let it dry until it's only a bit malleable (leather dry). Place a large, smooth stone in the concavity and paddle the outside of the vessel with a flat piece of wood, to compress the walls of the pottery and help eliminate air bubbles. Set the pottery aside to dry for weeks, or longer, and then fire it. You can learn more complex pottery production techniques, like coil pottery, after learning the basics with these "pinch pots."

221 GET FIRED UP

Firing the pot is the next hurdle in working with this ancient technology. Once dried mud has heated enough to become ceramic, it can never dissolve in water. Follow these steps to minimize the chance of a making broken pottery shards.

STEP 1 Let your proposed pottery dry for weeks to eliminate all but the bonded water; otherwise you risk cracks, breaks, or violent explosions.

STEP 2 Preheat gently; dry pottery can still explode if exposed to thermal shock. Gradually warm it and turn the item near a fire to preheat it.

STEP 3 Once preheated, encircle the object with a ring of burning sticks and then push them closer to the pot *slowly*, over the span of an hour. Once the pottery is very hot, gently place sticks over it and bury it in coals to fire it thoroughly.

STEP 4 Let the pottery cool down completely before moving it from the dead ashes of the fire. Inspect it for cracks. If none are visible, flick it with your fingernail. If it rings like a bell, you did a good job. If it doesn't, you can still use it, but it may not last as long.

222 PEEL SOME BARK

Ever notice how easy it is to knock off a chunk of tree bark in late spring? Every year, the bark loosens before the tree adds another growth ring. This is the perfect opportunity to peel tree bark for crafts and projects. Long before the invention of metal pots, and even before ceramics, bark containers have been used worldwide for cooking and storage. From the birch bark buckets of the Native Americans in the Northeast to Aboriginal bark cooking pots in Australia, the containers have been as diverse as the people who have made them. Today, peeled tree bark can still give us strong and versatile vessels to use for our own survival.

Bark can be collected in late spring and early summer across much of the world. Select a young tree with thin bark. If you can, cut the tree down and drag it out. In a primitive survival scenario, you can use a stone hand axe as a bark chopper to remove the bark without cutting the tree down. If you've cut the tree down, cut around the tree in two places, then score a line parallel to the trunk which connects the two cuts. Mimic those cuts while the tree still stands, if you are using a stone chopper. When you've finished your cuts, wedge a stick or a chisel underneath the bark and carefully peel it free. Once the bark is off, you can flatten it and dry it for later use, or better yet, use it immediately to make a container.

223 BEND A BERRY BUCKET

Getting the bark skinned off the tree in one piece is typically the worst part of making a container, and for most people, it's not that bad. When it comes time to actually make the container, it's often easier than you might think. A great bark basket to try first is my favorite, commonly known as a "berry bucket." You can make this bucket style short and wide to act like a basket, or long and slender for a nice arrow quiver that's already camouflaged to match the local forest (nothing blends in with bark like more bark). The only limits are the flexibility of the peeled bark and your creativity.

STEP 1 Scratch or compress a football shape on the inside center area of your freshly peeled or thoroughly rehydrated tree bark.

STEP 2 Etch this shape in the middle of your bark, with the "points" of the football just touching each edges of the bark. Fold the bark in half, allowing the scored section to bend freely.

STEP 3 The shape you made will bend inward, and the cylindrical vessel will be complete when you tie the bucket together with cord or rope.

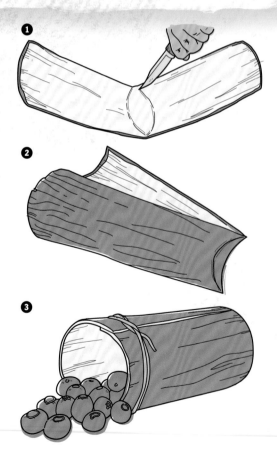

224 MAKE A COOLAMON

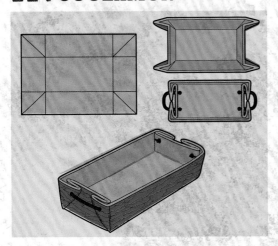

If you don't crack the bark, this unique dish is waterproof due to the watertight nature of intact bark and the strategic positioning of the edges. Follow these steps for a traditional bark coolamon.

STEP 1 Peel a very thin and flexible sheet of tree bark, with no knots, holes, or visible defects.

STEP 2 Using the side of a spoon, an antler tine, or some other hard, smooth object, scribe a square into each corner of the inside of a soft bark sheet. Then scribe a large rectangle connecting some of those lines to define the bottom of the container.

STEP 3 Scribe an angle line through each of the four "corner squares," angled from the center of the bark sheet to the outside corners.

STEP 4 Gently bend each of your scribed lines to soften the bark without breaking it. Then fold the bark along those lines. Drill small holes in the bark to "stitch" the corners in place with cordage.

STEP 5 Use the coolamon to transport water, as a box for storage, or as a rock-boiling vessel. If you plan to keep it watertight, treat it like a wooden bucket. Keep it filled with water or submerged in water while it's not in use, to prevent cracking which would ruin the piece as a water vessel.

225 BUILD A BARK TROUGH

I have tried a lot of different container tricks and experiments over the years. Few have left me as satisfied as this "trough" idea. So if the bark is peeling but you're still having trouble assembling a rock-boiling vessel for primitive water disinfection, give this a try.

START WITH BARK AND PLUGS Collect a sheet of bark and two large, round, smooth river cobbles. If the rocks aren't smooth and round in your area, cut disks of wood from any log with no end cracks. The plugs should be large enough to leave a slit in the side of the container that is one quarter of the "tube" circumference. Once you've picked your plugs, place one of these plugs at each end of the bark and get ready to apply some torque.

FINISH WITH TWO TOURNIQUETS Put a smooth rock on each end of a fresh-cut bark trough and wind an improvised tourniquet around each end. Some bark troughs drip a little more than others, but overall the technique will work. If you plan to have windlass sticks underneath, they act as runners to keep your trough sitting stable.

underside

226 PREP YOUR HIDE

Animal skins can be transformed into several types of material—each one suitable for many different things. Fresh skins that are dried (with or without the hair) produce rawhide, a very tough, stiff form of leather. Skins can also be oil tanned or vegetable tanned to become flexible leather. With the right amount of work (and some brains), skins can also be brain tanned for the softest leather. However you intend to finish hides, there are certain things you'll need to do to prepare them.

CUT THE FAT The most essential part of your prep work is called "fleshing," which is the removal of meat and fat from the hide. Meat will rot, leading to decay of the skin. Fat goes rancid, and also contributes to decomposition. You'll need to scrape all of the meat and fat off the hide, as thoroughly as possible. If the hide has just been peeled from a fresh kill, the meat and fat can be scraped off the skin and thrown into a soup or stew. If the hide has been lying around for hours or longer, use your scrapings for trap or fish bait. Fleshing can be done in different ways, but I prefer to scrape with the square edge on the back of a drawknife handle, while pressing the hide against a smooth log for support.

FREEZE OR DRY Raw fresh hides can be stored for years in a deep freezer, or kept outdoors in subfreezing climates. If storage conditions are above freezing, your best bet is to dry the hide for storage. Put the fur side in the sun, either loose or stretched out in a wooden frame, since any remaining fat will melt if the sun hits the flesh side. Dry until the hide is stiff, and you have "rawhide." Once a hide is dried, it can be rubbed liberally with salt, or better yet Borax, all through the hair side. Borax (sodium borate, available in the grocery store in the laundry section) won't stick to the dried flesh side, but will settle into the fur to discourage insects that would eat holes in the hide. The hide can then be stored flat, hung up on a wall, or rolled up into a tube.

227 SOFTEN A PELT

Long before tanning solutions, our forebears used the naturally occurring oils in the animal's brain. All you need is an animal hide, the brain of the animal, and a few other items to tan pelts just like our ancestors.

DRY AND SAND After fleshing and drying, sand the flesh side of the pelt with sandpaper until velvety, to make it more receptive to the brains.

MAKE BRAIN SOUP Use your blender to blend the brain along with warm water, using the Liquefy setting, or mash the brains by hand in a quart (1 L) of water. The resulting liquid should be the consistency of hand lotion. Boil the solution for a few minutes, then let it cool to the touch before bringing it into contact with the skin.

GET TO WORK Lay the pelt on a flat surface and work the brain solution over the skin by hand until thoroughly covered. Dampen a towel and wring it out. Roll the skin up in the damp towel and set aside for a couple of hours. While still slightly damp, begin stretching the hide in all directions to break up the skin and soften it. This may take one hour or several, depending on pelt size and thickness, as well as the humidity and air movement around the skin.

HAVE A SMOKE Smoking a tanned hide won't waterproof it, but keeps it from stiffening if it gets wet and dries. Suspend the flesh side of the hide over a small pile of embers and rotten wood chunks. You don't want flames or much heat under the hide, just smoke. When the color of the flesh side has changed, that's enough smoke.

Leather pouches can be made in many different ways to hold a myriad of items. These are just a few of your options.

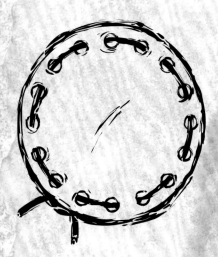

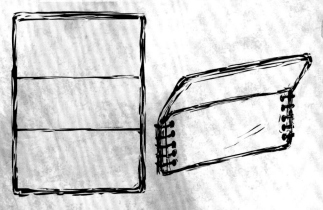

SEW A THREE-FOLD POUCH Cut out a long rectangle of leather and use a bit of charcoal to mark lines dividing it into thirds. Fold over one third and punch holes down the sides that are touching. Stitch these two sides together and the extended third of leather will act as a flap to close the pouch.

CUT A ROUND POUCH On a round or oval disk of soft leather, slice or punch holes around the perimeter. Run a length of lace or cord through all of the holes, going up through one hole and down through the next one, until you've made the circle. Pull the cord tight to close the pouch and create a pouch shape.

STITCH A BALL BAG This design makes a nice ball bag for black powder shooting, as the pouch can stand up when it is full or partially full. Cut a small, round disk of soft leather, and a rectangular piece which is the same length as the circumference of the leather disk. With a needle and thread, stitch the rectangle into a tube, and stitch the disk onto the bottom of the tube. Add drawstrings by poking a few holes near the opening of the bag and threading a leather lace through there. Then you're done!

9 BUSHCRAFT USES FOR MUD

From humble origins comes an unexpectedly versatile substance. Mud may seem nasty and valueless, maybe even troublesome, but this is all just a matter of perspective. This squashy form of dirt can become many different things in the hands of a creative survivor. Here are nine ways that mud can help you in a survival scenario.

❶ **MAKE CHARCOAL** If you need some charcoal for a simple forge or water filter, mud can help! Build a cone out of tinder and kindling, surround it with chunks of hard firewood, and then build a mound of mud over the woodpile. Leave a hole in the mud at the top of the kiln and one at the bottom. Light up your tinder at the bottom and let the kiln catch fire fully. Plug the two kiln openings with more mud once the fire is burning well, and the mound will snuff out slowly over the next 24 hours. Break it open when it's cool and harvest your charcoal.

❷ **BAKE FOOD** Mud can make a surprisingly effective cooking wrap for many foods. Wrap an apple in clay-rich mud and bake it in a bed of coals for 1 hour to make a sweet baked apple treat. Pack mud around a fish and bake it in the embers until the fish is flaky, moist, and perfect.

❸ **MAKE AN OVEN** Pack a mountain of mud over a bundle of sticks, leaving a hole for a chimney and a door. Allow this mound to dry for a week or two, light the sticks on fire, and you have a brand-new clay oven.

❹ **SET A CAST** Use alternating layers of mud, fabric, and sticks to create a temporary cast for an injured limb. Start by padding the limb heavily for comfort with this heavy cast. Encircle the padding with blunt sticks, making sure that none of the sticks are poking your patient. Start applying mud and strips of fabric. Don't be skimpy with the fabric strips; this really holds the mud together and adds strength to the dried cast. Allow the cast to dry and keep it dry. Then let the cast do its job of stabilizing the injury.

❺ **LOSE YOUR SCENT** Trapping animals is a subtle art, and scent plays big role in your success. Remove the human scent from your hands (and even from trap parts) by wiping them with mud.

6 CRAFT CERAMICS Mud with a high clay content can be formed into an almost limitless array of ceramic items. Blend together one part crushed stone and two parts clay, then work the material until well blended. Make a clay pot by shaping the tempered clay and then letting it dry before firing in a campfire.

7 SHAPE A BOWL The technique of coal burning—slowly using hot coals to hollow out a hardwood bowl—is very effective, but sometimes it eats away too much of your raw material. Wiping mud on the wood when coal burning creates a fireproof barrier to prevent "over burning" your project.

8 MAKE MORTAR Need to secure some stones to make a hearth or even build a rock wall? Mush together mud and dried grass or other fibrous material to create a sturdy mortar. As I write this, I'm sitting near a century-old wall that still contains remnants of mud and horsehair mortar.

9 CAMOUFLAGE YOURSELF Nothing compares to mud for natural camouflage. Smear mud all over your exposed skin, clothing, gear, and anything else you need to conceal. Pat some debris, dust, or vegetation onto the mud for even better results. For the fastest application, wallow in the mud and then roll across the dry ground. You'll feel silly, but you'll end up matching your surroundings perfectly!

229 WATERPROOF YOUR BASKET

In a primitive survival setting with no tools to help you, one of the hardest things to acquire can be a waterproof container. Thankfully, a few big handfuls of mud and some sturdy basket vines can give you a temporary solution. Weave a tight basket (any style you like), and line it with a thumb-thick layer of clay-rich mud. This messy basket will hold water immediately, though it will cause the water to become very muddy. And if mud-flavored water isn't your thing, there are two ways to get around it. For immediate help, stick little flat stones in the mud inside the basket. Get them tight, like a jigsaw puzzle, and this will limit the amount of mud that can enter your water. Option two is to let the mud basket dry completely (a few days to one week). Once dry, fill it with twigs and light them on fire. This will harden the surface of the clay and the smoke will offer a mild waterproofing.

PRIMITIVE SKILLS

So far, you've learned many different skills to keep you safe and comfortable in the wild. What about the heritage skills that support these endeavors? It's hard to craft a fire kit without tools to saw out the notch or put a point on your drill, and harder to tie knots without cordage, or put a stone blade on a handle without glue. This section is full of skills, wilderness tricks, and outdoor information too valuable to ignore.

230 MAKE QUICK STONE BLADES

An easy way to get sharp stone blades is a method called bipolar percussion. There are three rocks involved: You strike a small rock (trying to break it) with a medium sized stone, while holding the small stone atop a big stone.

BECOME A STONE SMITH Imagine you are a blacksmith. Your biggest rock a placed on the ground and acts like an anvil, in order to provide unyielding resistance underneath the rock you want to break. You'll also stand up the rock that you want broken on its tallest axis. Make it stand tall, as if you were trying to make an egg stand upright. This is a highly important part of the process, because it allows the shock waves from the hammer stone strike to move through the rock on the longest path. Once the stone is stable and ready, use your medium–sized hammer stone to crack down hard on the small rock. The hammer rock should be four to five times larger than the rock you are trying to break. If you're lucky, you'll fracture off some nice, thin, wickedly sharp stone blades within a few strikes.

STAY SAFE WITH STONEWORK For any stone tool work, make sure you wear gloves, preferably made from leather. You'll also want to wear glasses or goggles of some sort, to protect your eyes from stone chips.

231 | USE THE SIMPLEST TOOLS

When you think of the primitive tool kit our ancestors used, it's easy to fixate on more sophisticated tools like flint knives and stone axes. But long before humans made complex tools, they must have recognized the humble tools that they could make out of the rocks and natural features all around them.

I find that I use a simpler and more foundational tool set for most of my work in a primitive camp. These unmodified stone tools and an ordinary fork in a tree could be used to work and process wood and other materials to create a variety of supplies and new tools. All it takes from you is the ability to spot these resources and a little finesse in using them.

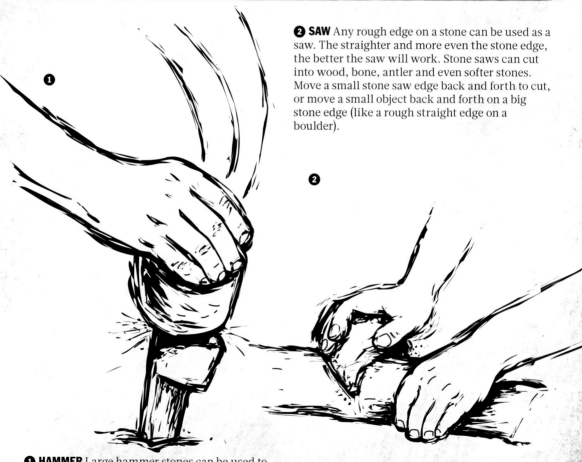

❷ SAW Any rough edge on a stone can be used as a saw. The straighter and more even the stone edge, the better the saw will work. Stone saws can cut into wood, bone, antler and even softer stones. Move a small stone saw edge back and forth to cut, or move a small object back and forth on a big stone edge (like a rough straight edge on a boulder).

❶ HAMMER Large hammer stones can be used to break sticks or drive stakes into the ground. Small to mid-sized hammers could be used for a wider range of tasks, from pounding tinder to pounding in wedges to split wood, from cracking open shellfish to chipping shapes out of other stones.

❸ SANDER Rough stones can be used as natural sandpaper, rasps, or files. Flat stones can grind down flat surfaces. Rounded sanders can get into concave areas.

❹ CHOPPER A sharp edge on a stone can act as a chopper or cleaver. This can cut or damage wood so that it can be broken with leverage or with a hammer. One handheld chopper used against the edge of a boulder can act as "shears" to cut wood or other materials from both sides at once.

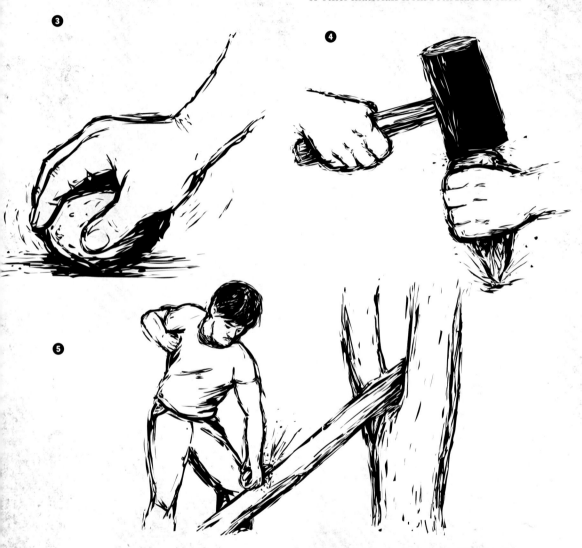

❺ LEVERAGE When you have a fork in a tree, or two trees very close together, you have the perfect place to use leverage to break wood. Insert the piece of wood, at about the height of your hip if possible. Walk forward, pushing against the wood with your hip; if it's not too thick, the wood will break at the fulcrum point. This doesn't work very well on thick hardwood or short sections of wood, but longer pieces of wood should give you all the leverage you need to break them. For a precise break, use a stone saw or chopper to damage the area you want to break, and make that spot your fulcrum.

232 SOURCE SOME STRING

Cordage is one of the most indispensable items that a person can have in the outdoors. Cord can tie together a shelter, build traps to get meat, bind tools to their handles, be used as fishing line, and perform countless other necessary tasks. Cordage can be easily made from countless fibers in tree barks and plant stems. Get to know these fiber sources, and you'll always be able to make string.

INNER BARK Many trees produce fibrous inner bark for raw material for cordage, after harvesting from dead branches and tree trunks. Bark can also be stripped from live tree trunks and branches, and soaked in water for several days, in a process called retting. Check the fibers daily until they separate from the outer bark. Twist them into cord wet or after drying, or use them as-is.

PLANT STALKS Several plants can produce usable fibers for cordage after the stalks have died and dried out. Many of these plants (aside from dogbane and others) are available for cord only in the fall, breaking down as they weather.

LEAVES Some leaves can be torn into strips or twisted into rough cord. Some leaves like yucca can have fibers retted. Others, like cattail, need special processing. Cut the leaves of cattail while green, and dry them in the shade. After drying fully, wet them and twist them into cord.

233 MAKE YOUR OWN STRING

Once you have a good collection of materials, you can then use them to craft plenty of your own string or cordage.

STEP 1 Get started by collecting the strongest fibers you can find. This may be flax or hemp that you have grown, or fibrous inner bark, or wild plant stalks like dogbane.

STEP 2 Grab a small length of fiber and begin twisting it. Continue twisting until it kinks. Hold the kink, and keep twisting each bundle of fiber.

STEP 3 If you twisted clockwise to begin the cord, then keep twisting the fiber bundles clockwise, yet allowing them to encircle each other counter clockwise. It is the opposing force that makes the line strong.

STEP 4 Meticulously splice in new fibers to continue twisting for a long length of cordage.

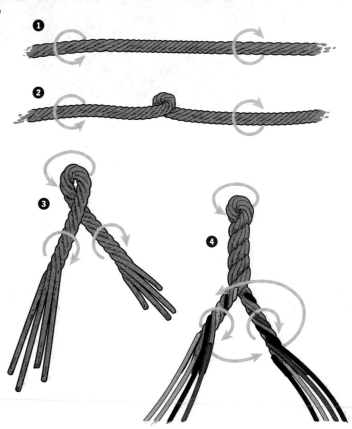

234 USE HIDE GLUE

Hide glue is a strong all-natural adhesive. This type of glue has been made for thousands of years worldwide, from scrapings or de-haired scraps of mammal skin, sinew, tendons, de-scaled fish skins, de-feathered bird skins, and many other animal parts. Hide glue is great for attaching bindings on tools and arrows for use in dry conditions. It can handle heat, but will melt if wet.

PREPARE YOUR GLUE The fibrous proteins, called collagen and elastin, are extracted from the animal parts (called glue stock) by cooking them in water without boiling. Temperatures over 180°F (82°C) will break up the proteins, weakening the glue. The strongest glue can be made by simmering the stock between 130°F and 150°F (54°C and 66°C). Each part of glue stock should be simmered in two parts of water until swollen and gelatinous, which takes several hours. Replace any water that evaporates during this process. When finished, filter out the glue stock remnants by pouring the mixture through a cloth, and squeeze any liquid out. This "glue water" can be simmered until it has a maple syrup-like consistency, and is ready to use at that thickness. However, it will not keep in this state, and must be dried for storage, or it will rot. The two best ways to dry the glue are as a glue stick and as glue chips.

SAVE GLUE STICKS Once your glue is ready, with a clean small stick, spin up a little glue on the end of the stick. Blow on the glue, and it will cool and gel. Continue to quickly dip the glue stick end into the glue syrup, and blow on the growing glob to gel it. If you can't get much or any on the stick at first, either let the glue cool some more or simmer longer to thicken it. When the stick looks like a lollipop, set it aside to dry. The glue ball will shrivel up to half its beginning size as it dries over a few weeks, but this simply means the glue is being concentrated. To use the glue again, just dip the glue stick in warm water, and the glue on the outside will reconstitute and be ready to apply.

MAKE GLUE CHIPS You can also cool your glue syrup until it becomes a gelatin, then slice it up into sheets and thoroughly dry it. The dried glue chips can be reconstituted by simmering them in a small amount of water; again, you should not let the glue boil.

235 BREW SOME PITCH GLUE

Pitch glue is a waterproof resinous glue made from the sap of evergreen trees such as pine, spruce, fir, and cedar. It is ideal in wet conditions but melts easily in heat.

STEP 1 Gather sap and pitch from open spots on evergreen trunks and branches. Clearer, softer pitch is best; dark, harder pitch has impurities, but is usable.

STEP 2 Select a vessel that can become the glue pot, because you'll never get all of the glue out of it again. Heat the pitch you have gathered in the container to about 200°F (93°C), at which point the turpentine and volatile oils evaporate. Pitch hardens at temperatures under 100°F (38°C), and liquefies at hotter temperatures. As the sap cooks, the gases coming out may catch fire; keep a lid handy for your vessel, and simply cover the glue and the flames will go out.

STEP 3 Once "cooked", the pitch can be used as-is, or charcoal dust can be added for up to half of the volume to make the glue less brittle, and stretch your supply. Pitch glue hardens as it cools, so the objects you intend to glue must also be hot, or the glue won't stick properly.

236 TEST OUT A TORCH

To make a torch that looks just like the ones on the silver screen, you can use the same oils as a grease lamp. Keep in mind that torches are for outdoor use only and that hot oil may run down the torch handle, so wield yours carefully.

STEP 1 Gather your materials: 50 feet of toilet paper; half a cup (4 ounces) of any cooking oil; and a green-wood stick about an inch in diameter and two feet long. The stick must be green; if it's dry the torch head will burn through and fall off.

STEP 2 Wind the toilet paper around the end of green-wood stick. Spin the toilet paper a little so that it ends up looking more like white rope, as you wrap it onto the stick. Tie an overhand knot with the end of the paper as it runs out. The torch should look like a giant Q-tip when done.

STEP 3 Soak the paper-covered end of the torch in the oil for a few minutes, absorbing as much as possible.

STEP 4 After soaking, you can light the torch at any time with an open flame. It will take about 30 seconds to light, but soon the entire torch head will be engulfed in flames. The average torch will burn about 20 minutes, and provide enough light to read.

237 MAKE A CANDLE

Candles have been an important light source for millennia. Although candles are susceptible to the wind and they represent a fire hazard, they're just too valuable to ignore. Here's how to make them, if you happen to have a bit of wax and string.

DIP A TAPER Dipping your own wax candles is really easy, and all you need is paraffin and cotton string, or better yet, beeswax. If you have your own hives, you'll naturally have leftover wax from your honey collection. Beeswax candles burn several times longer than the same-size paraffin candles. Melt the wax down to a liquid in a deep container and start dipping a cotton string into it. Dip the string once and pull it out to cool and harden. Dip it quickly again to thicken the wax skin without melting off the previous wax layer. Keep repeating this quick dip and long cool process until you have the desired length and diameter of candle. By using a long string bent over double, you can make two at once, and have that cool "pair of candles on a string" like you see in old-timey stores.

ROLL ONE OUT If you don't have much wax to work with, there is a simpler technique than dipping. Wax can be melted on a flat surface, peeled up in strips and simply rolled up into a cylinder shape. Roll them around a plant fiber string, and you'll have your wick right in the center—exactly where it needs to go.

DON'T BREAK THE MOLD To make the nicest candles, you can pour melted wax into molds. Traditionally, candle molds were made into specific shapes, but virtually anything can act as a mold. Use cups or cans to receive the melted wax and insert a wick once it gels but before it hardens. Once rock hard, pull out the candle and it's ready to use.

239 FIRE UP THE FATWOOD

Large splinters and sticks of fatwood are great fire starters in wet conditions and when kindling is scarce. These sticks are also very handy as primitive lighting instruments. Stick some pieces in the ground and then light them up for bright little torches. For an even brighter burn, you can tap your knife into the end of a fatwood piece, splitting it slightly, and then wedge a sliver of fatwood into the bottom of the split to hold it open. Repeat the split on a perpendicular bias to make a four-pronged torch, which will give you a bigger flame that sheds even more light.

238 GRAB A GREASE LAMP

Excess or rancid grease and oil can be used as fuel for a very nice lamp when coupled with a plant-fiber wick and a fireproof container. Here are just a few options you can combine to create a light source, and the steps to make it happen.

CHOOSE YOUR OIL Almost any liquid or solid oil is fair game for grease lamps and oil "candles." People have used lamps for millennia, fueled by lard or tallow, and plant oils—most notably olive oil. You can also use paraffin lamp oil, vegetable oil, or used cooking oil. Pure olive oil or paraffin burn the cleanest, with the least smoke.

FIND A VESSEL Large seashells, clay bowls, or even metal lamps can act as a container. Glass food jars also work well, since they can handle heat. Whatever the container, it should sit stable on the ground as well as on any flat surfaces, and should be fireproof.

ADD THE WICK Select some kind of plant fiber (cotton and jute work great, but any natural plant fiber will work). Fill your container with about an inch of whatever oil you're using as fuel. Light the wick with an open flame, and you're set.

9 BUSHCRAFT USES FOR ANIMAL FAT

When you're first learning to butcher wild game, those gross whitish blobs of fat seem like refuse. But a more seasoned survivor knows that fat is, in some situations more valuable than the meat itself. Whether the fat is right off the animal and still warm, or you've rendered it into lard, this important resource can serve a wide range of bushcraft uses.

① FIRE STARTER Wipe a little lard onto some tinder and light it up for a wet weather fire starter that burns with a strong heat for several minutes. You could also apply lard to wood, charcoal, or any other flammables to help them burn better and longer.

② FORGE QUENCH Warm liquefied animal fat, or even cold solid lard, is a great quench "fluid" for knives, tools, and other forged objects that need to be hardened. The fat quench is gentler than water—in fact, pig fat was widely used on the early American frontier. An animal fat quench also creates a food-grade protective coating.

③ LAMPS You can make a "snowball" candle out of raw animal fat by just squeezing it into a ball, inserting some plant-fiber twine to act as a wick, and lighting it up. For the more sophisticated survivalist, fill a fireproof vessel (like a clay or stone bowl) with rendered lard and add a wick to make a primitive grease lamp.

④ WATERPROOFING Leather boots and other outerwear become less permeable to water with a healthy coating of animal fat. Mountain men, hunters, and trappers once wiped animal fat on their thin leather moccasins to keep them soft and somewhat waterproof. Smear it on thick over stitching and seams, and you too can buy some time before the water comes through.

⑤ SOAP Rendered fat can be blended with lye and water, then stirred until slushy, and set aside for aging to create homemade soap.

6 LUBRICANT From black powder rifles to friction fire sockets, animal fat can provide an excellent lubricant on metal surfaces. It also inhibits rust on iron and steel objects.

7 MEDICINAL SALVE Healing plants can be dried and soaked in warm lard to create salves and balms. Dried yarrow leaves make one of my favorite salves, which can help to stop minor bleeding and reduce the risk of infection on cuts, scrapes, and scratches.

8 CONDITIONING Dry cracked skin can get a healing boost from a light rub of animal fat. Your parched leather boots and gloves could benefit from a wipe of animal fat too. And how is your hair so shiny and soft? Bear fat.

9 CALORIES Fats are the densest source of calories, and every calorie can count in emergencies. If your animal fat is still "food grade" (read here: not rancid yet), use it for cooking or simply add a little bit to other foods to spike up their calorie content.

240 RENDER ANIMAL FAT INTO LARD

Animal fat can be a challenge to store. In temperatures above freezing, your valuable fat can quickly go rancid. Thankfully, there is a way to store fat at warmer temperatures without spoiling too fast. This method is called rendering, and it involves cooking the fat for a long time at low temperatures, then filtering before storage. Here's how.

STEP 1 Cut the fat into small cubes, and remove all meat, veins, and non-fat tissues.

STEP 2 Drop the cubes into a pot with a little water in the bottom, then bring the fat and water mixture to a low simmer, trying to stay under 150°F (66°C). If the water starts to boil, the fat will burn when the water is gone. Simmer for several hours.

STEP 3 When it seems like all the fat has liquefied as far as it can go let it cool just a little, then pour through a cloth to strain it.

STEP 4 Simmer the fat for about another 30 minutes, and filter once more for the best shot at a long shelf life.

STEP 5 Pour the final filtered fat into small jars or cans, and keep it in a cool dark place. It should last a few weeks in warm summer temperatures, or a few months in the colder weather. And if it starts to smell bad, you can still use it for a non-edible purpose.

241 TRACK A PERSON

A trail of human footprints. Are these simply a collection of imprints and shapes in the soil? Or are they something more? For thousands of years, our ancestors have tracked animals by the various footprints and other sign that they leave behind. And they have also tracked their fellow humans. Whether they did so to find a lost child, or some darker end, the rules and techniques of tracking were the same. And while its roots reach back into antiquity, human tracking still serves valuable purposes today. Here are just a few of them.

FIND THE LOST Both children and adults can become the target of search and rescue missions.

Having skilled trackers on the ground can bring a happy conclusion to many of these stories.

BACKTRACK YOURSELF Lost your way? Instead of continuing to wander, follow your own tracks backward to a point of familiarity. Though this is easier said than done, it's still a viable possibility for the observant outdoorsman.

DO SOME SCOUTING Military and law enforcement personnel have the upper hand when using solid human tracking techniques to learn about the movement and numbers of the people that they are observing.

242 FOLLOW THE STEPS

The fastest way to get into this field of study is to start tracking yourself, or better yet, track a friend. They can even circle around and join you at the starting point, so you both can look for tracks. Two sets of eyes are always better than one. Take your time, and look for the following clues..

LOOK FOR LUGS Most modern outdoor footwear is designed for traction, with lugs on the outer soles to grip the terrain; these diverse shapes are unmistakable from animal tracks.

FIND THE RHYTHM Without a change in speed or terrain, distance between footprints often stays the same. Once this distance is figured, you can predict where the next footprint will be.

PICK THE PATH When terrain doesn't show all tracks, look for natural features that would steer a person in a certain direction. These could be gaps between boulders, trees, thorn bushes, or other blockades. Check the space between each opening to pick up a lost trail.

SAVE THE TRACKS Walk next to the known tracks and give a wide berth to areas with unknown tracks, so you're not inadvertently stepping on the tracks you're trying to find.

243 TRACK WITH THESE TRICKS

Whether you are searching for a lost person, backtracking yourself, or simply want to see how many people went down the trail ahead of you, tracking can provide answers. It's part science, part woodcraft magic, and all observation. Here are some basic tips to get started.

WATCH FOR TRACK TRAPS Sandy or muddy depressions are a hoard of information for a tracker. The larger and damper these beds, the more complete your picture becomes. Avoid stepping in these, to keep a lower profile yourself.

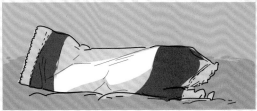

LOOK FOR LITTER Intentionally discarded items (like trash) or items that have been accidentally dropped are a great indicator of someone's presence, and these items may give you clues about the person.

LOOK FOR AERIAL SPOOR Tracking should always include the observance of signs above the ground, and never just prints in the dirt. Classic sign, like broken branches or snapped spider webs, can tell us that something passed that way.

DON'T FORGET THE TARGET Whether you are tracking a lost child or a trespasser on your property, don't get so focused on the tracks and trail that you forget about the "thing" at the end of the trail.

USE ALL YOUR SENSES Most people track by simply looking for footprints, but sound and scent are of value too. Stop and listen to the environment now and then, and smell the air. You may hear your quarry moving if they are near, or pick up the smell of deodorant, perfume, cologne, or food.

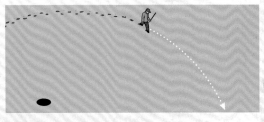

REGAIN THE TRAIL Odds are, you'll lose the tracks at some point. Most trackers retreat to the last known sign, then walk a 4- or 5-yard (4- to 5-m) circle, carefully scanning for new sign. You could also follow the most likely line of travel to see if you can pick up the trail.

244 BRANCH OUT

Learning to track is like learning a new language. It is a stealthy script, written since the dawn of time, and it gives us a glimpse into the secret lives of animals all around us. Not only does animal tracking give us clues about the animal population and behavior in a given area, it also lets us stay away from predators and locate prey. Whether you are a hunter or just an observer, tracking can even have a major impact in a survival situation. Get to know these two branches of animal tracking.

KNOW THE SIGNS Sign tracking can be used in most environments, and in some terrains, it's all you'll have. This method involves tracking by following signs, marks, disturbances, and leavings of an animal. From trails to piles of scat (the technical term for animal poop), sign tracking demands that we look for more than just footprints in the dirt, sand or snow.

CLEAR THINGS UP Print tracking is what most people associate with tracking. It's the art of finding and following footprints on the ground. Some surfaces are ideal for holding clear prints. Wet snow and damp sand are excellent for holding tracks, while hard packed dry soils and shifting dry sand are very difficult to track on.

245 LEARN SOME PATTERNS

If you're looking to hunt an animal in the wild—or to stay clear of one—an important part is knowing the tracks they make. Some can be awfully similar, but to a practiced eye, there are noticeable differences. This chart should give you some idea of what to look for in some of the most commonly mistaken critters out there.

TRACK PATTERNS

white-tailed deer

moose

dog

coyote

red fox

gray fox

bobcat

lynx

house cat

otter

fisher

mink

weasel

raccoon

striped skunk

porcupine

beaver

black bear

opossum

woodchuck

muskrat

snowshoe hare

cottontail rabbit

gray squirrel

white-footed mouse

crow

turkey

ruffed grouse

Animals leave behind a lot more than just footprints. Trails, beds, rubs and chews can give a general idea of the species that are present. Hairs, feathers and droppings can tell us exactly which animals are nearby. Looks for these signs and you'll be much more aware of your surroundings.

LOOK FOR TRAILS AND RUNS These signs are equivalent to highways and side roads. Some trails are used by many different species, while runs are typically used by just a few animals or even just one species. Trails are usually not a great place to set traps, since larger animals may just knock them down. Runs are better suited for trap placement.

SPOT A FEEDING AREA These places are species-specific and seasonal—berry patches, grassy areas, open spaces, most any spot that can provide nutrition. By examining the actual chews in a feeding area, we can also make an informed guess about the animals using it. Clean cuts and gnaw marks are made by rodents, while serrations are made by deer; vegetation torn and pierced full of holes has probably been chewed by a sharp toothed predator (like the way a dog or cat chews grass for fiber and minerals).

FIND A BED Animals that don't make nests (like deer) often bed down in fields and thickets. Some beds are used only once, and can be seen as an oval depression in the vegetation. Repeat-use beds show a greater disturbance. Some animals only make beds in thick vegetation to better hide from predators.

LOCATE RUBS AND SCRATCHES Commonly found along trails and runs, rubs are places where an animal will rub against a tree or some other object. They may do this to scratch themselves or in order to mark the territory with their scent.

WATCH FOR HAIR AND FEATHERS When deer rub under low hanging vines and branches, you can sometimes find hairs stuck in the rough bark. At an animal rub, you may also find a spot where hair gets snagged. Beds are another site to look for hairs or feathers, and of course, kill sites will have clumps of hair or feathers from an animal that was devoured.

247 KNOW YOUR COMPASS PARTS

There are several different types of compasses available to the outdoorsperson today. They range from tiny "button" compasses that you might find in a survival kit, to complex compasses with loads of features you'll never use. For the average bushcrafter, an orienteering (aka baseplate) compass is a great choice. These are the parts and here's how they work.

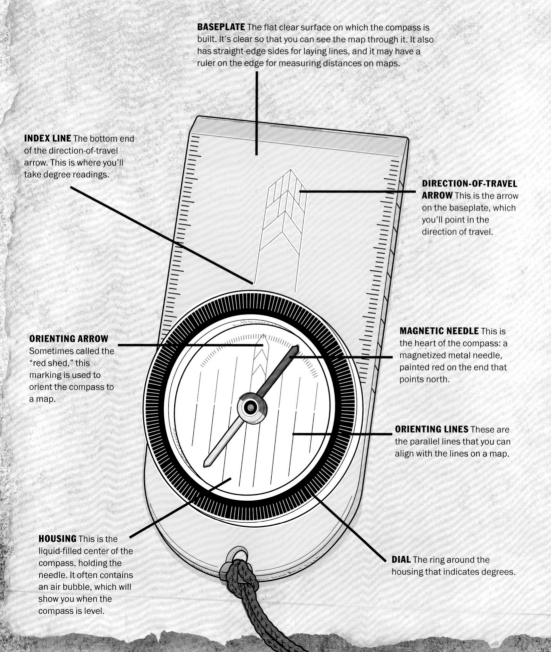

BASEPLATE The flat clear surface on which the compass is built. It's clear so that you can see the map through it. It also has straight-edge sides for laying lines, and it may have a ruler on the edge for measuring distances on maps.

INDEX LINE The bottom end of the direction-of-travel arrow. This is where you'll take degree readings.

DIRECTION-OF-TRAVEL ARROW This is the arrow on the baseplate, which you'll point in the direction of travel.

ORIENTING ARROW Sometimes called the "red shed," this marking is used to orient the compass to a map.

MAGNETIC NEEDLE This is the heart of the compass: a magnetized metal needle, painted red on the end that points north.

ORIENTING LINES These are the parallel lines that you can align with the lines on a map.

HOUSING This is the liquid-filled center of the compass, holding the needle. It often contains an air bubble, which will show you when the compass is level.

DIAL The ring around the housing that indicates degrees.

248 FIND TRUE NORTH

One of the main reasons that novice map readers get confused is the fact that there are really two "norths" to consider when looking at your map and compass together. True North is used when maps are made and illustrated. It is the actual geographic North Pole and the spot where all longitude lines converge. And it's a real shame that your compass doesn't usually point that way. The needle of your compass is drawn toward Magnetic North, and the difference between these two is called declination. Based on your location, you'll have to add or subtract a certain number of degrees to accurately turn the Magnetic North reading of your compass into True North to orient your map (and yourself). So if you're in Maine or Washington state, your compass might be about 20 degrees off from True North. Don't worry. All contemporary topographical maps show the degrees of declination, and it's not as hard as it sounds at first.

249 MAKE YOUR OWN COMPASS

The earth is a giant magnet with a large magnetic field around it. If a magnetized needle can spin freely, it will align itself with this magnetic field. And if you've lost your compass, or you didn't bring one in the first place, you might just have the materials to make one. Improvising a compass can be especially important in overcast weather, thick forests, or other conditions that eliminate most direction-finding techniques.

STEP 1 Take a needle or a bit of steel wire, and then rub a magnet repeatedly against the needle, going only in one direction. Rub the magnet about twenty to thirty times against this prospective compass needle you're creating.

STEP 2 Set the needle in a curved leaf in a water-filled container (or larger leaf filled with water).

STEP 3 Block it from the wind completely; if all goes well, the needle should swing into a north-south alignment. Now, you will just have to figure out which is which.

250 READ A MAP

For most people, the only maps they look at are flat road maps. But topographic maps can show you a 3-D world in 2-D.

SEE ALL THE DETAILS "Topo" maps show contours of the land like valleys and mountains. Topo maps even show waterways, vegetation, trails, roads, and other details. But by far, their best trick is to show the shape of the landscape, to better help you travel in it.

FOLLOW THE ELEVATION Contour lines connect points of equal elevation. When contour lines are spaced far apart, the landscape is relatively flat, and when the lines are tight together, it's steep terrain. On every topo map, the contour lines are spaced by even increments of elevation change, and your map will reference the elevation. Just check the margin of your map to learn the distance intervals, or do some quick math to see how many feet or meters the map is using as intervals. With practice, you will see all the shapes that a 3-D sculpture of the terrain would show.

251 SET UP SHADOW STICKS

Can't figure out your directions, but you know it's midday? The sun still gives enough info at midday if you use a sun compass (or "shadow stick"). Just stick a twig into soft ground in an open area that is receiving direct sunlight. Then place a stone or make a mark on the ground at the point where the stick's shadow ends on the ground. The sun moves east to west at about 15 degrees per hour. After about 2 hours, make another mark to record the tip of the shadow again. The first spot you marked a few hours ago is your western mark, and your new mark is the eastern point. Lay a stick on the ground or draw a line between the marks from the shadow tips; and you have established an east-west line. Add small stones to mark each hour of the day and you'll have a sundial to tell time (and you still have your compass).

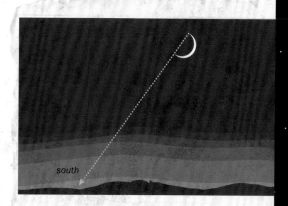

south

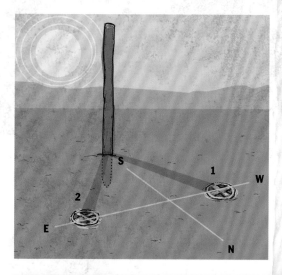

252 FIND YOUR WAY WITH THE MOON

Just as the sun moves from east to west, so does the moon. Due to the moon running on a different schedule than the sun, it may not be rising or setting at a convenient time to assist your navigational needs, but at least it follows a similar path. And that's not the only way that the moon can give directions. The crescent moon is a shape recognized around the world, but few people realize what the "horns" of the moon are telling us. When the crescent moon is high in the night sky, use a straight stick (or just your imagination) to make a line that touches each tip of the "horns" and extends down to the horizon. This spot on the horizon will be roughly south (for those in the northern hemisphere). If you're trying this below the equator, the line passing by the horns and extending to the ground will show a rough northerly position. This trick also works when the moon is in any other phase (except the full moon, obviously).

253 DON'T BELIEVE THE MOSS

You may have heard that moss always grows on the north sides of the trees. I'm sure this might be accurate once in a while, but also remember that a broken clock is still right twice each day. Depending on the climate, latitude, moss species, and a host of other factors, that moss can grow anywhere it likes. Don't rely on this one for pathfinding.

255 LOOK TO THE SOUTHERN CROSS

When early European sailors first sailed south of the equator, they were no doubt dismayed to see their guiding star (the North Star) disappear below the oceanic horizon. But they soon learned that the northern stars had a counterpart which could give them a southern bearing. Sometimes called Crux, the Southern Cross can help you establish which way is south in the southern hemisphere. Just draw an imaginary line between the top star of the cross (Gacrux) through the bottom star (Acrux) and down to the horizon for a general bearing for polar south. You can use an imaginary spot between the two "pointer" stars left of the Cross and the Cross itself to draw a line straight down toward the south pole.

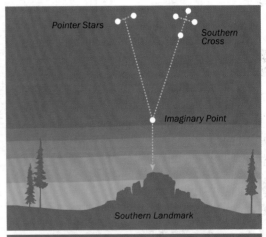

Pointer Stars

Southern Cross

Imaginary Point

Southern Landmark

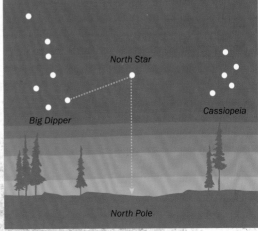

North Star

Big Dipper

Cassiopeia

North Pole

254 FOLLOW THE NORTH STAR

Most folks can find the Big Dipper (Ursa Major) in the night sky. And if that was all you could find, it would give you a general idea of north for those in the northern hemisphere. But for a more precise way of finding your bearings, follow the two stars on the side edge of the dipper's cup until you hit the dim star "next door." This is Polaris, the North Star. It gives you a very accurate bearing toward True North. If the Big Dipper doesn't happen to be visible at your location or time of year, the W-shaped constellation of Cassiopeia can help. It is on the other side of Polaris from the Big Dipper. It's also possible to find Polaris by finding the Little Dipper (Ursa Minor).

HEALTH & HYGIENE

Hygiene is not just a social nicety, it is vital to the health of individuals and groups. There are few things as vile as having a gastrointestinal bug tear through camp—or worse, pathogens leading to more serious infections. Luckily, these sanitation issues can be prevented with just a little conscientious behavior. Whether you're in a survival situation or on a family campout, here's how to keep clean and safe.

256 WASH UP

You can stay clean and healthy in the wild without modern plumbing, soaps, and scrubbing tools. Here's how.

SIMULATE SOAP Certain plants naturally contain soapy compounds that can bubble up and clean your skin when mixed with water and a scrubbing action. Ensure you are using a safe soap plant by checking it out thoroughly in a good field guide.

Various leaves, roots, and flowers from plants such as yucca or clematis can be crushed in a little water to produce suds. Test a small amount sparingly at first to see if you're allergic, don't get lather in your eyes, and never try unknown plants, as they may carry toxins.

SCRUB AWAY Even without anything sudsy, you can scrub with sand or cedar boughs, and rinse with water to remove dirt and dead skin cells. The cedar will leave a slightly antibacterial oil behind (along with a better smell). You can also get some cleaning results with dry wood ashes.

Rub your hands with white or gray *dry* wood ashes and then rinse thoroughly. Don't use wet wood ashes or mix wood ashes in water for washing, as the mixture releases lye, which will cause chemical burns.

WASH WELL If you have water nearby that is not a drinking source, you can use your soapy materials to wash your hands and even take a bath. If the body of water isn't big enough for you to submerge in, splash up water as best as you can. Don't bathe in or near a drinking source, and stay downstream of where you draw up water for drinking. Don't get water in your mouth or up your nose, to help avoid getting sick if you're bathing in contaminated water.

257 LIGHTEN YOUR LOAD

When you've got to go, avoid contaminating your camp and the surrounding environment. Have a designated place to go, to keep a great deal of dangerous bacteria out of your camp. If the population of your camp is low, you may want to just to use "cat holes" for short term disposal of solid human waste. Use a trowel, digging stick, or the heel of your boot to dig a hole in the ground, a bit larger than your predicted deposit.

SUBSTITUTE FOR TISSUE The best toilet paper substitute can be found in the winter or at high elevations: packable snow. Snowballs can make excellent toilet paper. They wipe and wash as you go, leaving no residue other than moisture. The next best thing is a stack of dead leaves with a green leaf in the middle (for structural integrity). Following that are bundles of fibrous inner tree bark or bundles of dead grass. Even rounded stones can work in a pinch. Lastly, ensure you know what poison oak, poison ivy, and poison sumac look like, and don't use them! Some fuzzy leaves (like mullein) may look perfect for toilet paper, but they cause a rash.

KEEP IT ALL COVERED Fully cover your waste when you're done, and then place a cone made of sticks over the top after you've buried everything. This temporary marker will keep you and others from stepping in waste, but will have fallen down by the time that your "night soil" has been fully decomposed and turned into real dirt.

258 GET DOLLED UP

You may not associate deodorant, nail care, and haircuts with primitive living, but there's no reason these things have to disappear in the wild.

BEAT BODY ODOR Deodorant isn't just a social nicety; it's a hunting tool. That's right: the more a hunter stinks, the easier it is for the animals to smell the hunter. Thankfully, nature provides us with deodorant. The common cleavers (*Galium aparine*) grows in the woods and along transition areas from spring through fall. This plant can be boiled and eaten as a wild edible plant, and the water can be cooled and applied as deodorant. The cooking water seems to suppress bacteria, giving you some extra time before you begin to stink after bathing. For year-round use, some powdered charcoal applied to the skin is great for absorbing odors.

GET A HAIRCUT Sharp stone flakes can be used to cut long hair. Hold hair taut, and cut on the tension side of your fingers with your stone flake, instead of hacking at the loose hair.

DO YOUR NAILS Speaking of fingers, you can also use a small abrasive pebble as a fingernail file. Employ it regularly to keep your nails short, instead of waiting for them to get long. Long nails are a breeding ground for bacteria and other dangerous organisms, so keep your nails as short as you can.

259 DON'T FORGET DENTAL CARE

Have you ever been caught out in the field without your toothbrush? Thankfully, there's a heritage version that we can still use today, and you can even make your own floss and toothpicks.

Ⓐ BRUSH WITH PINE Grab a tuft of pine needles, and give your teeth a good scrubbing. The needles leave your breath fresh. Just skip the loblolly pine in the American Southeast, and the ponderosa pine in the American Southwest, as these two species may have a little toxicity.

Ⓑ POUND A TWIG To make a twig toothbrush, simply cut a green twig about the diameter of a pencil and just as long. Pound the end of the twig with a clean, smooth rock. Then chew this end for a minute to moisten and soften the bristles; and

finally, brush away. Skip potentially poisonous twigs like mountain laurel, rhododendron, black locust, yew, buckeye, and horse chestnut.

Ⓒ TRY FLOSSING Nontoxic cordage fibers from plants such as dead, dry stinging nettle inner bark, or other strong plant fibers can be used as floss. Select fibers that don't break apart easily, to avoid having broken fibers stuck between teeth. Animal fibers (like dried strips of sinew) and long human hair can also be used as floss.

Ⓓ PICK YOUR TEETH Dull thorns or splinters are fine toothpicks. If you poke your gums and they begin to feel tender, rinse your mouth with boiled acorn water for a few minutes at a time, a few times a day, until the irritation subsides.

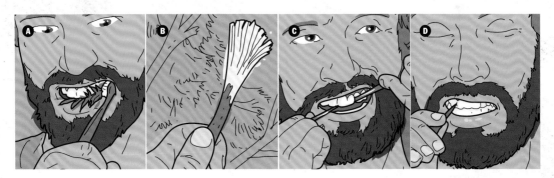

260 SAY HI TO AUNT FLO

Being a dude, I can't speak on this topic with the greatest of authority, but it's still an important issue to consider. Feminine hygiene items date back further than you might imagine. Ancient Greeks and Romans made tampons by winding clean cloth around small sticks, though this is hardly advisable. Some Native American cultures, among others, used pads of tanned hide filled with absorbent fibers or moss such as sphagnum moss for menstrual pads. These pads were washed, dried, refilled, and rotated as necessary. They were typically rectangular pads,

open on one end, resembling miniature pillowcases. These pads were held in place with strings or cord.

If you don't have the leather or cloth to spare, or don't have any sewing skills, then just a bundle of nontoxic, absorbent material can be used by itself. Whatever you use, you should be very cautious about scent in bear country, or other remote areas with large predators or pack predators like wolves. Don't leave the pads or used fillings lying around to draw any wild animals' attention.

261 BUILD A MEDKIT

By purchasing a ready-made medical kit, you are much more prepared for medical emergencies. By building your own medical kit, you'll have the best chance of having the specific gear you'll need to survive a medical emergency.

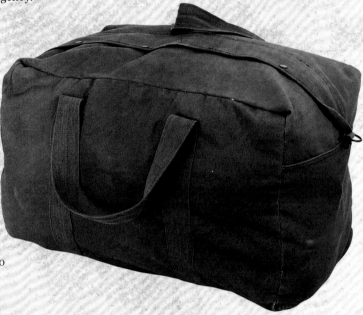

+ SPACE BLANKET Wrapping a patient can help fend off shock or help with hypothermia treatment.

+ NITRILE NON-LATEX GLOVES (5 PAIRS) Protect yourself from pathogens. Use nitrile or plastic gloves, as many folks are allergic to latex.

+ TWEEZERS For removal of splinters, ticks, or foreign objects from wounds.

+ TRAUMA SHEARS These can cut away clothing and belts to give you access to wounds.

+ 8X10-INCH (20X25-CM) TRAUMA PAD This sterile dressing can stop bleeding on a large area.

+ 4-INCH (10-CM) ISRAELI DRESSING A wraparound bandage that can be tightened to add pressure and stop bleeding.

+ QUIKCLOT ACS This treated sponge causes rapid clotting to stop serious bleeding.

+ TOURNIQUET In case of severe bleeding on a limb, this can constrict the blood flow.

+ TRIANGLE BANDAGE Useful as an arm sling, a dressing, an improvised tourniquet, and many other things.

+ 20 ANTISEPTIC WIPES Disinfect wounds and your hands.

+ STERILE SALINE EYE WASH (8 oz / 240 ml) Use this to remove debris or chemicals from the eye, or to irrigate wounds.

+ EYE PAD Use these to dress eye wounds, or any other small wounds.

+ 2 ACE BANDAGES Use ones with Velcro ends, for pressure dressings and to bind orthopedic injuries.

+ 4 ROLLS OF GAUZE Control bleeding, dress wounds, and much more.

+ 6 4X4-INCH (10X10-CM) NONSTICK GAUZE PADS These can dress wounds, especially burns.

+ 40 ASSORTED FABRIC BANDAGES Use these on the boo-boos that don't need a tourniquet.

+ 1-INCH (2.5-CM) MEDICAL TAPE Keep a roll to keep all your nice dressings in place.

+ 2 AMMONIA INHALANT SWABS These can revive someone who's fainted.

+ 1 TUBE EACH OF ANTIBIOTIC OINTMENT, ANTI-ITCH CREAM, AND BURN GEL Use these to treat various wounds and ailments in the field.

+ IBUPROFEN OR OTHER NSAIDS Carry a bottle of these pills to relieve pain or inflammation.

262 MAKE A POULTICE

A poultice is about as old-school and simple as it gets. You're just smashing up a plant and applying it directly to the problem area. This is used primarily on external problems, but it could be held in the mouth for gum or tooth problems, if the poultice material is nontoxic. To make a poultice, crush (or even chew) the plant material into a pulp or paste, and apply it directly. Keep it in place with a bandage or some other type of dressing. Replace it with new material once or twice daily, until you no longer need it. Plantain is one of the best poultices for wounds, especially insect bites and stings. Some people report relief in mere minutes once applied. Other great poultice choices include curly dock root, comfrey root or leaf, and yarrow leaf.

263 CREATE A CAST

A broken wrist or a fractured forearm may not be a killer, but can be excruciatingly painful and a major impediment in the field. These injuries need to be stabilized and supported to reduce the pain and limit further damage. If you can't get out of the backcountry to the doctor or there is no access to medical care in a disaster, you can try a very old technique: the mud cast.

❶ **FIND SOME MUD** Check out riverbanks and other wet areas for clay that is moist and ready to go. Test the quality of the clay by rolling the mud into cigar-shaped pieces and bending them. The more they flex without breaking, the better they will work for the cast. You'll need about 1 quart of clay-rich mud for a forearm cast, and more mud for bigger casts.

❷ **WRAP THE LIMB** Rolled gauze is a great medical item, but any cloth will work for the initial limb padding. Wrap strips of cloth around the injured limb and add a few sticks for stabilization. Wrap over the sticks to keep them in place. Put a ball of cloth or gauze in the hand to pad it as well. Place the wrist in a "position of use," which means the back of the hand is slightly lifted.

❸ **MAKE LAYERS** Begin to add a layer of mud over the cloth, and add additional strips of cloth. Rolled gauze is excellent for this, as the mud will squish through it. Add more layers of mud and fabric until the desired size and shape are reached (roughly the size and shape of a normal cast).

❹ **USE A SLING AND SWATH** For any arm casts, improvise a sling from available materials or use a cravat. Place the arm in the sling and allow the cast to dry. For additional support, you can tie a long bandage around the entire limb and torso (swath). Once the mud has dried, this crude but effective cast will be much heavier than a modern orthopedic cast. However, it is very supportive and can be made from available materials in almost any location.

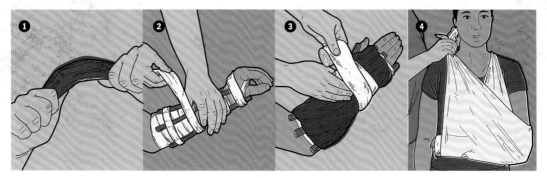

264 FIGHT THE COLD

The human body comes equipped with hundreds of features for survival, though few are as important as the mechanisms that combat heat loss. The cold is one of our oldest adversaries, but as we have developed better and more effective clothing, we have reached a point where we are no longer as vulnerable to exposure as our ancestors once were.

Even with the advantages of modern clothing, the cold still kills people every year. Lost hunters and hikers, the homeless, the poor, and the unlucky succumb to exposure from cold temperatures each winter. And this number would be lot higher if it weren't for our body's automatic response to reroute blood flow.

LET YOUR BODY ADJUST We don't have to say any magic words or flip a switch. When our skin and extremities get cold, the body reduces the blood flow to these areas. This will reserve more warm blood for the vital organs in the body's core and the brain. Of course, there are drawbacks to this system. If we are not careful, the reduced blood flow to the skin will make frostbite more of a possibility (in subfreezing conditions). But overall, this cold response saves more lives than frostbite takes.

265 STAY HYDRATED

The human body constantly loses water to its environment and through metabolic processes, so we need frequent "refueling." When that's not available, the body starts saving water. Urine becomes darker and more concentrated, and the output diminishes. Our blood thickens and our waste becomes harder and drier. Dehydration causes headaches, a lack of strength and energy, constipation, cramps, and a host of other symptoms. But this mode of operation can save you from death by dehydration. The best way to track your hydration is to keep track of your water intake and urine output. You should be taking in more than 2 quarts a day, and urinating at least a quart and a half each day. Factor in exertion levels, stress, health, weather, caffeine, and other factors, but if you are peeing every few hours, your body won't have to shift into the water-thrifty setting.

266 SKIP SOME MEALS

Fattening restaurant meals and an increasingly sedentary lifestyle have taken their toll on the world's waistbands, though it's not entirely our own fault. Our bodies are still exhibiting traits they picked up during ancient times, namely the ability to "pork up" during times of plenty.

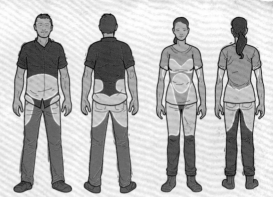

KEEP THE CALORIES Long ago, a little fat around the middle was our own private and portable famine insurance system. That's right, the "spare tire" is the body's mechanism to prepare for the inevitable pattern of feast and famine. The only problem is that first-world countries have virtually eliminated famine, thanks to production farming and globally reaching food chains. Your body is still expecting a failed crop or the lack of game animals that our ancestors experienced on a regular basis. When that doesn't happen, you just keep ballooning.

WATCH YOUR WEIGHT DROP But as soon as we step back into nature, the body starts burning fat. Especially when we are in colder air, the body uses its stored calories for fuel. Even when we have food to eat in the wild, the pounds start melting away. And if no food or inadequate food is available, then the body still knows what to do. It starts burning fat and consuming other tissue. In this catabolic state, the body is essentially eating itself. If adequate water and shelter are available, this process can go on for weeks (or even a couple months, if we were particularly beefy). So bring food with you into the wilderness, and learn how to procure food from the plant and animal kingdoms—but don't freak out if you miss a few meals; your body knows what to do.

267 STOP BLEEDING

Injury is one of my greatest fears in the outdoors. It's so easy to cut yourself while carving with a sharp knife, or slip up when swinging an axe. And with edged-tool injury comes blood loss. Even if you're not squeamish about blood, it's scary to see large amounts of this precious life fluid spilling all over the ground. Thankfully, there are ways to stop bleeding and compensate for blood loss.

LET THE BODY WORK Through many complex reactions, your body can detect injury and blood loss. When this occurs, severed blood vessels may contract, growing shorter temporarily, which decreases the size of their unnatural opening. Blood platelets begin to clot and muscles stiffen, which is thought to be the body's attempt to immobilize the injured part. The heartbeat (pulse) can increase to allow the remaining blood to make up for the missing blood. All totaled, the human body has an amazing response to injury and blood loss.

ADD A HELPING HAND In serious cases of bleeding, direct pressure should be the first tool for bleeding in your wilderness medicine toolbox. Apply generous pressure to the wound site with a dressing, a piece of clothing, or even your bare hand if necessary. Time is not your friend when someone's bleeding out, so don't worry about rummaging for sterile dressings. Infection takes weeks to kill, but blood loss can do it within minutes. Use a combination of direct pressure, elevating the wound above heart level (if possible), and improvised dressings. If a dressing soaks through, don't remove it. Just add another dressing on top and continue the pressure until the bleeding stops.

268 KNOW YOUR STRENGTHS

The art of survival doesn't begin when you start building a shelter or light a fire, but as soon as you get your head in the game. People with no skills, gear, or experience survive seemingly insurmountable odds and extremely deadly scenarios because they had the right mindset to avoid becoming a casualty.

While we never want to go into the wilderness without tools or training, people caught in that situation are not so empty-handed as they might think. Even if you're a rank beginner in the realm of outdoor skills (and even before you picked up this book!), you likely had some of the key elements survivors need to make it through an emergency.

That's right, even if you're caught without gear, you still have a "survival kit" that goes everywhere you go. This survival kit consists of your attitude, your mental toughness, your motivation to survive and your adaptability (just to name a few traits). And with these amazing survival tools at your fingertips, the average person is far more prepared to survive than they might expect.

269 STAY MOTIVATED

What motivates a person to live when everything around them has gone wrong? Survival stories are a testament to someone's devotion to their religion or higher power, something that motivated them and gave them hope. Other survivors have had an intense desire to get back to loved ones, family, or friends. Consider what would motivate you to stay alive through a brutal survival emergency.

It's different for every person, but on the long dark scary nights, it's the motivation to survive that really fuels a survivor. Hopelessness is the poison to motivation. If you lose the hope that you'll be saved and reunited with loved ones, if you believe God has abandoned you, or if you don't expect to get out of your predicament alive, then it becomes almost impossible to stay motivated and you are in a bad situation indeed.

270 ADJUST YOUR ATTITUDE

Just because "positive mental attitude" is mentioned in every survival book and wilderness class, don't discount it as cliché or lip service. Maintaining a positive attitude is a real necessity. I would even go so far as to say that it is a critical survival priority. A positive attitude in the face of adversity may be one of the most important skills to master. It is also one of the hardest skills to master. But it is worth the trouble.

A good attitude can foster hope, and allow you to look at the "brighter side" of a grim situation. You can also use this attitude every day, not just if you get lost in the woods. Pessimism is the opposite of our positive attitude. A pessimist will always see the bad side of a situation and often feel overwhelmed. To avoid this, suck it up and try to stay as positive as you can, while maintaining a firm grip on reality.

271 STAY MENTALLY TOUGH

We're not talking physical toughness, like your stamina, your muscle mass, or how many calluses you have. We are talking about the strength of your will and the toughness of your mind. This is not a tough body, but a tough head.

To be mentally tough, you must tolerate the intolerable, you must suffer through the insufferable, and you must overpower your weakness along with your desire to give up. Laziness can be a pitfall to your mental toughness. Survival is hard work and it can require some truly difficult choices to be made.

A survival scenario is not a vacation from your job, or some unexpected leisure time. Survival experiences, by their very nature, are tough situations. Taking the "easy way out" and being lazy will eventually get you into serious trouble. Be as tough as you can, and don't be lazy!

272 EMBRACE ADAPTABILITY

Adaptability and survival have always been closely related. Animals or plants that cannot adapt to their environments have died out; those who could, survived. To be adaptable, you must be able to adapt to changing events, situations, and environments. You must also be able to recognize when things are worth continuing or must be abandoned.

Stubbornness can occasionally be good, for example, being just too stubborn to die. But it can also hurt you, because it a refusal to change. It's simple to identify, but hard to correct. Maybe you were born stubborn, or your ego says you can't fail. But don't be afraid or too stubborn to change. If something isn't working, adapt! Don't let your stubborn streak kill you, or kill someone else.

A CASE FOR FEAR

Our instinct of fear, however unflattering, can be a helpful asset. We're all supposed to laugh in the face of danger and never get frightened, but that's just Hollywood brainwashing. We've all been scared plenty of times in our lives; the *right* amount of fear is a good thing. Fear can become our enemy in a life-or-death crisis—but it can also save us. Here's why fear is our friend, but panic is our enemy.

ACCEPT YOUR FEARS Our fear of heights keeps us from falling to our death. Our fear of snakes keeps us from getting bitten. Fear keeps us out of harm's way. When that fear is kept under control, it's working *for* us. But when we become overly stressed or fearful, we are at the mercy of the cocktail of hormones and chemicals in our bodies. It's quite common that this flush of hormones will lead to panic, which is definitely working *against* us.

DON'T PANIC! Panic can be described as unrestrained, illogical, and unthinking fear. You may run around frantically, or be frozen in fear and unable to move. You may even become overwhelmed by emotion, and start crying or screaming. These responses could get you into more trouble, and you'll have a new set of problems. But if you use your fear as a tool, and hold panic at bay, then you are the master of your fear (and not the other way around).

INDEX

FROM THE AUTHOR

This may be the end of the book, but my hope for you is that this is just the beginning of your education in the great outdoors. You and I are living proof that our forebears made a successful living by collecting their supplies and their meals from the wild, using a lifetime's worth of acquired skills. And while we may never achieve the levels of mastery that our predecessors once knew, we can strive to learn something new every day. Study your local ancient history, to find out how people provided for themselves in your home region. Learn from naturalists, to unlock the secrets of the plants and animals around you. Read everything you can get your hands on—and above all else, practice your skills! You'll learn from both mistakes and successes as you practice your bushcraft and primitive living skills, and your education doesn't ever need to stop. The late great outdoorsman Horace Kephart said it best: *"In the school of the woods, there is no graduation day."*

Thank you for reading.

ABOUT TIM MACWELCH

From growing his own veggies and raising livestock, to being a multiple *New York Times* bestselling author, Tim MacWelch is truly a modern day renaissance man. He is the author of *Prepare for Anything, Hunting & Gathering, How to Survive Anything,* and *The Ultimate Winter Survival Handbook.* He has also been an obsessed practitioner of survival and outdoor skills for over three decades, and he has been teaching the skills he loves for over two of those decades. Tim became interested in survival skills and woodcraft as a teen, while backpacking in remote areas he decided in would be a smart plan to learn some skills. The majority of his training has involved testing survival skills and devising new ones, but the biggest leaps forward came from teaching.

Tim has spent hundreds of hours volunteering with Boy Scouts, youth groups, and more as well as working with and training adults in all walks of life. Tim and his school have been featured on *Good Morning America,* several National Geographic programs, and in many publications including *Conde Nast Traveler,* the *Washington Post, Business Insider,* and *American Survival.*

Since late 2010, Tim has written hundreds of pieces for *Outdoor Life* magazine and many other publications. Tim's current and past articles and galleries can be found at outdoorlife.com and you can learn more about his survival school at www.advancedsurvivaltraining.com. When he's not teaching survival or writing about it, he lives a self-reliant lifestyle with his family in Virginia.

ABOUT OUTDOOR LIFE

Since it was founded in 1898, *Outdoor Life* has provided survival tips, wilderness skills, gear reports, and other essential information for hands-on outdoor enthusiasts. Each issue delivers the best advice in sportsmanship—as well as thrilling true-life tales, gear reviews, insider hunting, shooting, and fishing hints, and more—to more than 1 million readers. Its survival-themed web site also covers disaster preparedness and the skills to thrive anywhere from the backcountry to the urban jungles.

weldon**owen**

CEO Raoul Goff

VP PUBLISHER, WELDON OWEN Roger Shaw

ASSOCIATE PUBLISHER Mariah Bear

EDITORIAL DIRECTOR Katie Killebrew

VP CREATIVE Chrissy Kwasnik

ART DIRECTOR William Mack, Allister Fein

EDITOR Ian Cannon

DESIGNER Ian Price

PRODUCTION MANAGER Michelle Duggan

VP MANUFACTURING Alix Nicholaeff

Weldon Owen would like to thank Molly Woodward
for her proofreading expertise, and Kevin Broccoli
of BIM Creatives for the index.

ISBN 978-1-68188-762-3

10 9 8 7 6 5 4 3 2
2025 2024 2023 2022

Printed in China

OUTDOOR LIFE

2 Park Avenue
New York, NY 10016
www.outdoorlife.com

Outdoor Life is a division of Camden Media